For All Of My Life

The remarkable story of a woman's survival of abuse and her journey across the boundaries of, race and geography; ultimately though, this is a story of a mother's fight for her children.

Narrated by
Betty Jones to Vera Martin

Edited by Robert Jones

authorHOUSE®

AuthorHouse™ UK Ltd.
500 Avebury Boulevard
Central Milton Keynes, MK9 2BE
www.authorhouse.co.uk
Phone: 08001974150

First published by AuthorHouse 2/17/2009

ISBN: 978-1-4343-8622-9 (sc)

Printed in the United States of America
Bloomington, Indiana

This book is printed on acid-free paper.

" . . Betty Jones' survival of violence and abuse is less a testimony of strength, though it is that too, than a revelation of one simple but elusive quest: that she sought only to love and be loved. She leaves us with the belief that it is not expectations we must live up to, but dreams."

She sat before me
Face with a fragile beauty
Eyes dulled with pain
But yet from that
Radiated a sense of strength
Like the lion resting with the lamb
Solomon and Sheba
The skin pulled taut over the drum
A flame, which continued to flicker
In the strongest of winds
Determined to survive
For the sake of the children!

V.M.

Acknowledgments

This is book is dedicated to Betty's grandchildren:
Robert, Crispin, Michael, Ashley, Nikul, Ayanda, Paul
and all who follow.

A Poem for Nana

No light is brighter
No occasion more joyful
Than when I see you
You are like a star
Shining down
Showing me a clear path through life
I admire you
Respect you and love you

You are like a tree of knowledge
And no matter what they say
We shall never be apart
Our souls shall remain together
As you remain in my heart
And in my mind

(all my love. Michael. P.S. I miss you.)

For all of my Life was the working title that my mum used during the writing of this book. It is a curious title of which the meaning is unclear, changing the more one thinks about it.

The title contains an air of resignation, almost inevitability and yet as suddenly as this thought occurs, another, suggesting hope and possibility springs from the words. It conveys both looking back and also, somehow, looking forwards and yes, also inwards. Do the words speak of struggle, or search – or both? Perhaps the meaning is not unclear at all; perhaps Mum meant that *"For all of my Life"* should convey all of these things.

Mum died on May 8th 1997 aged 69 years. Although she never lost her love of living, the last twenty years of her life were dominated by debilitating illness and pain. Her ashes are buried with the mother she lost when she was a child of 12 – a deep, 'forever' kind of loss that never really faded.

My mum's mother, my grandmother, lay in an unmarked grave for over half a century and yet astonishingly, her whereabouts were revealed as if by magic in a search that took less than three hours. The place, 'Willow Grove Cemetery' is as its name suggests. Overgrown with willows and other trees, un-pruned rose bushes grown out of hand and spreading rhododendrons, closed now for some years – an overgrown place overrun with children who seem to find it a good place to play football, climb trees and ride bikes. It is noisy with children's laughter and squabbles. The children are right, it is a good place.

What the title *"For all of my Life"* suggests more than anything is continuity – not beginnings and endings, but a circular view of life. A spirit, 'other-place' connection that was powerfully portrayed in my mum's relationship with her grandchildren – the eldest member of the family in harmony with the youngest.

Betty, my darling mother, has journeyed home.

Adele Jones

Foreword by Vera Martin

This story is quite simply Betty's story. I have tried to tell it as it was told to me – simple and straight from the heart. It is a tale of immense courage and pain. Of struggle and survival. Like the African drum, its rhythm vibrates through the earth, its cadences touching hidden chords; the steady beat the sound of her survival.

On many an afternoon Betty and I met in her front room. In the peace and tranquillity of her cottage flat she told her story – a story so powerful that it needed to be written down. We talked about what she would like to see happen to the story once down on paper. It would be wonderful to see it in print. However for Betty it was a legacy she wanted to pass down to her children and grandchildren. It was something she wanted them to have and cherish and most importantly to understand. There were no real expectations of acceptance because she knew that her pain was her children's pain.

What she hoped for was their understanding – an understanding of her need to survive – for she believed her survival was their survival!

I was privileged to be part of this process – to be part of the storyteller's contact with her past! With respect I unfold her story in the great African tradition of story telling ...

Introduction by Robert Jones

The story starts where mum is alone and aged 20. Her mum and dad both died when she was still a child and the rest of her family disowned her for marrying a black man.

Despite this and despite the pain which was synonymous with her life, she remained strong and courageous. It was her dream for this story to be written. The realisation of this dream involved several people; beginning with mum herself, typing out the words on a small typewriter until arthritis wrecked her joints. She then moved on to use a recording machine and I was one of her typists in those early days - transcribing her words onto paper. But then even the recording became difficult and it was Vera Martins, a trusted friend, who made the telling of the story possible in the end. Vera, thank you, we are enormously grateful to you.

The violence and pain that mum endured throughout her marriage had transformed her once elegant frame into a bent and twisted body. Although racked with constant and daily pain, her mind and sense of humour remained. Despite the illnesses that beset her, she had the ability to bounce back and defy the doctors.

It was clear that through her courage and immense inner strength she would go only when she was ready to go, and when her role on earth was done. On the 8th May 1997, the day of the birth of Nikul, her youngest child's first born and surrounded by the children that she had lived and given so much for, it became clear that she was now ready to go.

As she states in her earlier poem "My children have grown one by one and now my work on earth is done ..." This book is, as she wanted, dedicated to her children, and her children's children.

Robert Jones

England; the early years ...

"**W**here do I begin? Sixty-four years old and so many things have happened to my family and me. Time is of no importance – Sixty-four or a hundred years, my life has no beginning or ending; it is a circle – a never-ending circle. Do you see that photograph on the side of the table?"

I looked over and saw a photograph of a tall young woman with a baby in her arms and three beautiful children by her side. The photograph was one of those old black and white photographs, which had been touched up with tinges of colour. The woman in the photograph was very attractive and had quite a presence emanating from her. As I stared at the photograph I saw that in spite of the slight smile on her lips her eyes had a kind of bleakness shadowing them. I looked at Betty and I still saw the presence without the physical resemblance.

"Yes," she said, "I am that woman. Look at me now – my body is racked over with pain, bent not erect, fingers twisted with arthritis – only a semblance of that young woman. I look at my children and the pain is of no matter – I feel so proud. Despite everything, they have survived – at least outwardly. Who knows what goes on deep inside of us, layers of pain and sometimes happiness so carefully concealed. The world only sees what it wishes to. I am proud of my children for in spite of everything each of them has achieved something special in their lives. My struggle for my survival should not have been their struggle and as God is my witness I never wanted it to be."

***

When I met Winston I was in the RAF. I had joined the RAF in order to get away from home and have some kind of social life. I loved dancing, going out and having a good time. Life was too short to be sitting around. I wanted to make the most of it, travel the world, meet people and perhaps, someday, marry and have a family. But believe me; marriage was furthermost from my mind. Life in the RAF was good. It gave me the chance to do some of the things I had always dreamed of doing. Sometimes if you work at it, dreams can become reality.

Winston and I met purely by chance. I sometimes wonder who rolled the dice – meeting Winston was like playing Russian roulette. We met on the tennis courts. Winston was playing and looked very dashing in his gear. At that time we were both based at Stafford. He was a good tennis player but if I am honest his tennis was not really what caught my attention. As I have already told you, he was very dashing; his physique and appearance were more impressive than the tennis. I must sound very forward but I guess honesty is more important. Winston was a good-looking man with a wonderful charming personality. We had a brief chat and I went off with my friends not thinking much more of him. That evening, a group of my girlfriends and I went to a dance hall in the town centre. I was in the bar getting a drink and who should be standing there —none other than Winston.

The chances of this happening were fairly remote so it makes me wonder whether our fate was sealed even before we knew it. I still wonder about who was rolling the dice for me! He offered to buy me a drink and we then seemed to spend the rest of the evening together. When I describe him as charming I am not exaggerating. I had a good time as he was great to be with and he was an excellent dancer. Needless to say, we arranged to meet up again and soon became dancing partners and friends.

Up until this point, life at the camp had been great. Lots of fun, lots of friends - in fact, I was quite popular. Once Winston and I began to be seen as an item things started to change. You have to remember that at the time it was unusual for a white woman to be seen regularly in the company of a black man. In fact I only now recognise how naive I must have been not to realize that I was acting in a taboo way. However it has never bothered me to do what other people feel is right. I have to follow my heart and conscience.

I did not see Winston as a black man – perhaps I should have! Anyway I was not so naive as not to notice the change in my friends, but if anything this made me more determined.

No one was going to tell me how to live my life. I can remember often being told by family that my stubbornness would get me into trouble. Little did I know just what kind of trouble! Need I say that I continued to see Winston? As you can imagine this really set the tongues wagging, and I put this down to small-mindedness!

Life at the camp got very difficult. I was put on extra duties so that I did not have a lot of leisure time. I guess this was to stop me from spending time with Winston. The authorities - C.O.,

Adjutant and the Padre all wanted to know how serious we were. The irony of all this was if they had just let things be, I would have got bored with the relationship and would probably never have married Winston. But there is little point in thinking about the 'what ifs'! I liked Winston and enjoyed his company. He had a way of making you feel special. Marriage, however, was just not on my mind.

I had volunteered to go to South Africa and wanted to experience as much of life as possible. However, with the authorities and the Padre going on at me, and telling what a bad reputation Winston had, this only made me more determined to continue with the relationship. Why, oh why, did they not leave us alone! You ask me why I was determined to persist with the relationship? You see I thought – no believed, that they were only picking on Winston because of his colour! I had plenty of reasons to convince myself that this was the case ... one night we went to a local pub with friends from the camp. When Winston went to the toilet, the landlord came up to me and said, "Are you with that nigger?"

I felt anger rising from the pit of my stomach and said in a controlled voice, "If you mean the coloured man, yes! I am with him. Why are you interested?" He then asked me to leave the pub. Even in telling you about this incident I can still feel the embarrassment, shock and anger that I felt. I can remember this overwhelming urge to protect Winston but also wondering why none of my friends spoke up for us. To this day I still carry the hurt and sense of being betrayed by people I knew and trusted. Every single person in the group had overheard the conversation and not one person stood up for me, let alone Winston. I did not want any trouble so when Winston returned from the toilet, I said that I was not feeling well and wanted to go back to the camp. To this day I wonder whether Winston had overheard the conversation or even knew what had happened! Incidents like these must have happened all the time to Winston but you know, we never talked about them.

* * *

At this point, Betty sat wearily back in her chair, her face looking strained. Quiet seemed to fill the room like soft balls of cotton wool muffling all sound. She then took a deep breath and said quietly, "Racism – I didn't understand it. I simply could not see how people could judge others simply because they looked different, or were of a different colour. It is only now through my children that I have some understanding.

"I have always felt that in telling my story, people would only remember that Winston is a black man. This story is about a man/woman relationship, it is about a stage in my life, it is about a circle which has no beginning or ending. This is not to deny that 'colour' had a part to play – but only as far as people's attitudes to Winston, the children and me. Now, where was I? Mm! Oh yes.

* * *

Much as I wanted to go to South Africa, Winston started putting pressure on me. He wanted to get married. Why? I don't really know. I would like to think that he loved me, but perhaps he wanted to prove something to the authorities. He started wearing me down. I was also fed up with the snide remarks and the pressure to end the relationship. I was also very stubborn and I refused to listen to warnings from friends, the C.O. and the Padre. I guess I questioned their motives and never really knew just how much they were influenced by issues of race.

Talking of warnings, another incident happened which should have sent me some warning signals. But, no, I was so convinced that people did not like Winston because he was black that I refused to acknowledge any problems. One night we were returning to camp from Stafford when another white woman came up to us. She must have been around 40 years old. She was very angry and started screaming and shouting, hurling abuse.

She shouted something like, "You do not know him. What he is capable of … he is a cheating …"

I felt so embarrassed that I wished the ground would open up and swallow me. I walked away and left Winston to deal with her. This scene really upset me and I tried to talk to Winston. However, as always he managed to sweet talk me around and reassured me that the woman was simply jealous. You know I never thought to ask him – jealous of what? He persuaded me that there was no way he could have had an affair with a woman so much older than him and that he only had eyes for me. I believed him, more fool I! Only much later, I found out that he had lied.

Getting married...

Friday 18th March 1950 – the date was set! I finally gave into the pressure and agreed to marry Winston. Little did I know what was in store for me! I sometimes wish we had a chance to look into some kind of magic mirror – a mirror that would help us to have some idea of the future.

However life is no mirror and we take our chances; the chance that I took almost destroyed me. In spite of his reservations, the C.O. was the only person who wished me luck, once he knew that we had set the date. On reflection, I think they were supposed to be good wishes –, what he actually said was, "I wish you the best of luck dear, because you are certainly going to need it." Famous last words!

The banns were published in Staffordshire Registry Office. At this stage the registrar contacted me to tell me that he heard that Winston was already married to a woman in Sierra Leone and that this information needed checking out. Again Winston managed to convince me that people were against our marriage because of his colour. I assumed that the registrar checked out the information because we were given the clearance in due course. This incident had now totally convinced me that people were desperate to stop us from marrying because Winston was black.

Three days before my wedding day Winston was arrested. Remember the woman who had hurled abuse at him? Well, it would seem that before we started going out, Winston had been seeing her and he had borrowed a lot of money from her. I find it difficult to remember the exact events and cannot remember whether she had accused Winston of stealing the money. What I can remember is my utter state of confusion – when was all of this going to stop? I just wanted to get on with our lives but it seemed like the whole world was conspiring against us.

Winston was being detained in the guardroom when I went to see him. He swore that there had been nothing between this woman and himself. There was an age difference of almost twenty years. It would feel like he was having a relationship with his own mother. He told me that he loved me and needed me to believe in him. He said that he had been framed and that everyone was against him because he was black. He begged me to stand by him and to marry him. I can see now that he played me like a finely tuned violin – a violin that *he* had tuned. And like the song goes, "I stood by my man!"

My friends tried very hard to persuade me to drop him and to cut my losses. I was confused, upset and just wanted some peace. I loved this man and I was going to stand by him – he needed me, but most importantly, for the first time I had someone who loved me. So I married Winston at Staffordshire Registry Office.

He was let out of the guardroom but remained under close arrest throughout the ceremony. Immediately after the wedding he was sent to Colchester to stand trial.

* * *

Betty leaned back in her chair and said in a tired voice, "And that was my wedding day. A day that every woman dreams will be special, a day to be happy; to have Champagne, cake and music. What I had was a short ceremony with a man I believed was innocent but with whom I could only say 'goodbye'. You know, there was not even a photograph of the wedding, not even one picture of what should have been the happiest day of my life!"

My family ...

With Winston in Colchester I decided to leave the RAF as a result of my bitter experiences. The RAF was my home and the only place that I could return to was Stockport. This was my hometown. I had an elder brother there who I thought might help me.

You might wonder why I have not mentioned my family up until now. You see I was never close to my family except for my brother, Joe. This was one of the reasons I had joined the RAF. However, I had kept in touch with Joe and he knew that I was seeing Winston. He did not approve and did not come to the wedding because he felt that I was making a big mistake. Joe did not know Winston; his main objection was based on the colour of Winston's skin. He did not actually say this but given my experiences to date, I don't think that I was far off the mark.

I got the train back to Stockport. It felt strange returning particularly after living in a RAF camp. I felt both exposed and vulnerable and knew that I was very much on my own – at least until Winston would be able to join me. As the train drew near Stockport I saw familiar landmarks and I had a strange sense of homecoming. Isn't that weird? I did not feel I belonged and yet there was a part of me that felt relieved about being in familiar surroundings! Of course by now I had no illusions about the struggle ahead of me. I guess the rose coloured spectacles had come off, and I saw the world for what it really was. Harsh, cruel and unbending – giving no favours or tea or sympathy!

My fingers were tightly crossed as I was hoping that Joe and his wife would let me stay with them until I found somewhere to live. I knew that finding a flat or rooms was going to be difficult particularly once Winston joined me. I hoped that if I had found accommodation before Winston came it would be difficult for a landlord/lady to evict us. Anyway as I got off the train I knew that I had nothing to lose at this stage and I made my way to Joe's house. My heart was thumping as I neared his front door because I honestly did not know what reception I would receive. Joe had been strongly opposed to me marrying Winston and had done everything in his power to stop the wedding. Joe did not know about the charges against Winston and I knew that if I was to expect any help, this had to be kept a secret. As I knocked on the front door I can still remember the feelings inside my stomach and how I had to hold my hands together to stop them from shaking. My worst fears were allayed and I was welcomed into the house but Joe was very upset.

I remember trying to talk to him but all he could say was, "girl, you have ruined your life!" Although I felt an enormous anger surging in the pit of my stomach, I had to bite my tongue. I was relying on their generosity and did not dare defend myself. To cut a long story short, after he had calmed down, Joe and his wife agreed that I could stay with them until I found my own accommodation. However they told me in no uncertain terms that they did not want Winston anywhere near the house. They would 'tolerate' my presence but Winston was not welcome. I simply cannot find the words to describe how I felt; I carried with me this sense of betraying Winston. Why could I not be strong in order to stand up for myself? Why did I let people talk or treat me in this humiliating way? I do not know the answer but I know that I was terrified of being homeless and destitute.

What about Winston? Had I any news from him? Oh, yes, I had heard from him but the news was not good. After a few days of arriving in Stockport I received a letter from him telling me that he had been found guilty and had been sentenced to eighteen months detention in Colchester. He wrote that an old friend from Sierra Leone, Johnny Smythe, had represented him. Johnny was also in the RAF but was studying law. At that time Johnny was only a name; little was I to know that many years later I would meet him in Africa.

What a way to start married life! I should have sensed that this was an omen of things to come, but you have to remember that from initially being ambivalent about marrying Winston, I now had convinced myself that I loved him deeply. Any doubts that I had I kept hidden like lava in the heart of a volcano, lava that was just waiting to erupt. I could not acknowledge these doubts as there were too many people waiting to rub my nose in it! Receiving Winston's letter put an end to my hopes of an early reunion. You know that I never really took it in that he had been found guilty. Like Winston, I believed that all this had happened simply because he was black and had dared to marry a white woman!

I felt so lost and alone. There was no one I could talk to – I did not dare let an inkling of the situation be known to Joe or his wife. I mentally tried to pull myself together and focus on practical things. I needed to get money in order to feed myself. I did not know whether I was entitled to marriage allowance with Winston being in prison. And I dared not ask! I just could not think of what I might have been entitled to! All I could think about was the shame. Given the circumstances I was in, I decided that the best thing to do would be to get a job, save as much as I could and look for somewhere to live. In those days jobs were relatively easy to get as long as you were not so fussy. I found a job in a machine factory and worked there for a few months.

* * *

Betty looked at me at this point. Pain and tiredness were stamped all over her face and body. I asked her if she wanted a break. We sat in a comfortable silence sipping cups of tea. She smiled at me and said, "This all sounds really bleak, doesn't it?"

I could not make any reassuring comments because anything I said would sound trivial and insensitive. We decided to break at this point and pick up the story at our next meeting. I went home feeling a sense of humility but also thinking; "This has got to get lighter – it cannot have been all so desperate. I must ask Betty if there were any happy moments."

At our next meeting Betty looked tired. However, she wished to continue with her story. I asked her the question that was bugging me. Was she ever happy?

Betty smiled, as if I had asked her if she had ever been to the moon. "Happiness, what is that? I am not sure. Oh, yes I had times when I was able to laugh and have fun with my work mates in the factory. And of course my love for Winston kept me going –the idea that one day we would live together was something that I looked forward to! However, I guess that fate or destiny had a few tough cards to deal to me."

* * *

Pregnant; No home, no money....

I had been at the factory for a couple of months when I started to feel sick. Regular bouts of vomiting convinced me that I was pregnant. I was pregnant! I felt an enormous flood of panic and despair. How bad were things going to get? Oh god, what on earth was I going to do? No home, no money, soon no job and no husband. What a mess I had got myself into! What would Joe and Josie say when they found out? Because as sure as hell, they would, in time find out. What would they do? Would they throw me out? I decided that the best thing to do was to say nothing until it became obvious to them. And then I started to worry about Winston – what would he say? That this is not what we had planned!

Then hardness came over me, tough! Nothing that had happened so far had been 'planned' – Winston was just going to have to live with the fact that I was with child.

The most important thing was to act as normal as I could. So I diligently went to work every day in spite of the persistent sickness. When I was being sick in the house I tried to do so as quickly as possible. Can you imagine, your insides are churning and all that you are worried about is being 'heard'! Again my naivety showed through!

Well, it did not take long for Joe to figure it out. Sure enough, one day on arriving home from work, I was just about to get changed, when Joe called out to me, "Betty, can I have a word with you?" My heart sank because I knew by the tone in his voice that my time was up. I tried to keep my face expressionless but it was hard. I was trembling inside.

Joe then said, "I don't want to pry, but Josie has noticed you being sick in the mornings; tell me are you pregnant?"

For a second a thought flashed through my head; brazen it out, but just as quickly I knew it would be pointless. How long could I keep it a secret? It was better that he knew and I decided to tell him the truth. "Yes," I said. "But I was afraid to say anything as I was frightened of losing your support."

Surprisingly, Joe took it very well and gruffly told me that I would be better off staying with them rather than being in rooms on my own. Words cannot express the sense of relief that came over me. However, I knew deep in my heart that this was a temporary reprieve. It was all right as long as the baby was not yet born but once the baby was born it would become a reality, and I knew that Joe would not be able to cope with having a black child in his home. Actually perhaps I was not being very fair to him. After all he had supported me against all the odds. But I had doubts about Josie and her views and she did have a strong influence on Joe.

I started attending the local clinic. The nurse there kept pestering me about the address that I was living at. I guess she needed it for her records. I did not want to give her Joe's address, as I really did not know what was going to happen once baby was born. Yes, I had started thinking of 'baby' rather than 'the baby'. I could feel baby growing inside of me and I really savoured this. I was frightened to enjoy baby too much in case fate decided to interfere. Going back to the nurse, I ended up telling her that I was staying with my brother and his wife but that I would need to move once I had the baby. I told her that my husband was a 'coloured man'. In those days to describe someone as black was seen as being insulting, 'coloured' was a more acceptable term. I went on to explain that because my husband was coloured, my family had been against the marriage. They were only helping me out temporarily until my husband could join me. I needed to find my own accommodation and as soon as I found a flat or rooms I would let her know so that she could book me in the appropriate hospital.

The months went by slowly and I still had not managed to find any accommodation. One day whilst I was out looking for a place to live, the nurse came to the house to find out where I intended to have the baby. Josie was there at the time. She told the nurse that it was not possible to have the baby from their address. When asked why? She made it clear that because Winston was black they were not prepared to have a black child in their home. After all, what would the neighbours say? So you see I had not been harsh in my earlier thinking that my time would be marked once the baby was born. I found out about the nurses visit from Josie herself. I guess she told me what was said to make sure that I had no illusions left. At the time I felt numb and did not allow myself to dwell on the incident.

However, the next day was not so good. I remember as if it were only yesterday, the intense feelings of loneliness and sadness. It was really hard to come to terms that I was very much on my own. My brother's support only went up to a point. I guess it was then that I started to realize that since I had made my own bed, that I was expected to lie on it. I knew that I and I alone had to somehow live with the consequences of marrying Winston. An overwhelming feeling to talk to someone came over me, and I felt that this had to be Winston; after all he was my husband and he needed to know what I was facing and to take some responsibility. I was weary of struggling on my own.

It was then that I made the impulsive decision to go and see him. Impulsive it was! If you remember, he was in Colchester at the corrective barracks serving an eighteen-month sentence. Even if I could get to Colchester, I did not know if I would be allowed to see Winston but I simply had to try. Desperation makes one do strange things! Once I made the decision to see Winston I made my way down to the coach station. I was told that I would need to get a coach to London and then another coach from London to Colchester. This journey was expensive and ate up the little money that I had. The journey was long – I think that I left for London at around lunch time and did not arrive there until the early evening.

By the time I got the coach to Colchester it was late so I arrived in Colchester really late in the evening. I had no money to stay overnight and knew that as soon as I had seen Winston I would need to make the journey home. To this day I do not know how I survived the trip. I suppose my utter desperation must have spurred me on!

As I had said earlier, I arrived at Colchester late in the night; it must have been around 9p.m. I asked for the directions to the camp and made my way there. I was exhausted and baby was kicking away furiously. I was determined not to leave until I had seen Winston. At the camp I found the officer who was in charge and asked to see Winston Jones. At first he refused saying that I needed official permission. I was so tired that I felt like shouting at him. I bit my tongue, swallowed my pride and pleaded. After all I had not come all this way to be turned away by petty rules! I must have looked a sorry sight, heavily pregnant, clothes creased from the long journey, face with lines of weariness. I told him that I was Winston's wife and had been travelling all day and would need to make the return journey later that night. I desperately needed to see my husband! He softened and finally took me to see Winston.

When I saw Winston I felt an enormous sense of relief and joy. It sounds strange talking about 'joy' and Winston in the same breath. But this was the man I loved; I had chosen to be with him against all the odds, a man who I believed had been unjustly treated by the authorities and his so called friends. I felt proud of my love and loyalty to him. It felt as we never had been parted because we quickly fell into our easy way of communicating with each other. Oh! It felt so good to unload all my worries, to talk about how I was feeling and to hold him again, even if it was only holding hands! I was surprised at how important touching him was, it made every thing seem real and not just some bad dream.

In a strange way it shook me out of my apathy and I knew the time had come to fight back. No one was going to hand out favours on a plate; we needed to take them.

At the time I did not think that he was really the source of all my difficulties and that ironically, he was being 'looked after' in protective surroundings whilst I was out in the cruel world struggling alone! If anyone had suggested this at the time I would have bitten of their heads as I was fiercely protective of Winston. To do anything less would be to admit that I had made a mistake and it was too early for that. Anyway my pride would not let me. Before I left to return to Stockport, I made Winston promise me that he would talk to the Padre to see if they would let him out on compassionate grounds. He needed to let them know that I would soon be having a baby, and that I had no real emotional or physical support.

Manchester......

I began the long journey home. Looking back now I think it was strange that once I decided to fight back, fate had now stepped in! Perhaps someone up there had decided to test my determination and me. On the coach I sat next to a woman who told me that she had a very large house in Manchester. When she said this, my brain went into overdrive. Here might be the answer to my prayers! I told her that I was looking for rooms and that it had been very difficult to find anything suitable. She immediately offered me the rooms in her house. I thought, "this is too good to be true! Perhaps I should test her further." So I told her that my husband, the father of my child was black. She did not bat an eyelid and told me casually that it was of no consequence. We parted company when the coach arrived in Stockport but made arrangements for me to visit her at her home.

On arriving at my brother's house I was so tired that I needed to rest up. After a couple of days I went to see Agnes the woman I had met on the coach. From the way she had described the house I was expecting something pleasant and grand. I was in for a big disappointment!

* * *

Betty looked at me and laughed. "I can see the funny side of it now but can you see how gullible I was, so trusting! People must have seen me coming".

* * *

Anyway this 'large house' was the last in a row of houses. All the other houses in that row had been knocked down and the area looked like a slum. Although all my dreams disappeared I decided that "beggars cannot be choosy"; I was desperate and for the first time, I had met someone who was accepting of Winston. So I went up to the front door and knocked! Agnes answered the door and looked pleased to see me and welcomed me in. Well, if I had thought that the outside was bad, the inside was decidedly grim! The hallway was dark and gloomy; the house was in such a state that I could almost imagine a dead body under the floorboards! I quickly tried to shake these unkind thoughts from my head. A desire to burst out laughing at this bizarre situation had to be kept under severe control. Agnes, very proudly, took me to see the two rooms that she was willing to let. One was up a flight of stairs and was a very dark looking room. The other was an attic room and was up a further two flights of stairs. This room looked dirty and had a bad smell, like something inside the room was rotting. Despite this, the attic room was very light. I felt with a good scrub it could be presentable.

You might wonder why I had decided to take one of these rooms – given the state that the house was in? I knew that I had to be realistic and this was the first person that had accepted my situation. If I waited to find something half decent it might never happen. Moreover Josie wanted me out of the house. Given these reasons I said that I would take the attic room and move in that week.

Six months pregnant, I moved into my very own place. Agnes let the room out as a 'furnished' room. Obviously with my situation I had no personal furniture. When I moved into the room, there was some kind of lino on the floor. It was so filthy that I could not make out the colour or design on it – that is why I described it as 'some kind of' lino. There was a marble washstand in the corner of the room, a fireplace and a double bed. The bed looked lumpy and smelt and it looked as if bugs might have made their home in the folds of grime in the mattress. If I needed the bathroom I would need to go down one flight of stairs – this was the only way to get access to running water. If I needed to use the fireplace I would have to buy coal and keep it in the back yard. My most valuable purchase at that time was a bucket. I could use it to carry water to my room and it also doubled up as a coal bucket! Small pleasures made my life so much more bearable! Anyway this was all mine.

When I moved in, I started cleaning. I spent the little money I had on cleaning materials – washed all the bedding, scrubbed the mattress, washed and dyed the curtains, and scrubbed and polished that lino until it shone. When the place looked habitable, I black-leaded the grate and got a fire going. I sat on the floor looking at the results of my hard work. With the fire burning in the grate, it threw a warm glow around the room and the room looked cosy. The glow spread; as it warmed up my tired bones I gently rubbed my stomach, whispering, 'I have now got a home for you, little one!'

I felt really proud of myself and felt some of my old spirit coming back.

Things started looking up for me. I began to attend the clinic regularly and knew that I had been registered to have my baby at Withington Hospital. I had also heard from Winston and the news was good. He said that the authorities were considering releasing him so that he could be with me at the time of baby's birth. He might have to return after the birth to finish his sentence but at least he was going to be with me for some of the time. For the first time since I had left Camp, I felt happy. Heavily pregnant, trudging up those stairs, I often sang to myself. On lonely nights I would gently stroke my stomach, talking to my baby, promising him all kinds of good things. I was feeling settled and had made my 'nest'.

As the time got nearer to having baby I went through a period of fainting. The hospital were concerned and decided to admit me until I had the baby. I enjoyed being looked after and it felt like heaven, not having to worry about mundane things. Just before I was admitted Winston was allowed home. It seemed as if my world had come together at last.

Winston warned me that he would need to go back once baby was born, but because of our circumstances he felt hopeful that he would soon be back for good. Winston visited me in the hospital every night and was so charming and caring. I could not wait to see him and anxiously counted the hours. Yes, I was very much in love and when our little boy was born, my happiness was complete.

Life with a new child...

The day came for me to leave the hospital with our newborn son. Winston came for me and I left on his arm, thinking 'how lucky I am'. When we got home and walked through the front door, the first thing I saw was my shiny new pram. I had been putting a few shillings away each week as I wanted my baby to have a new cot and pram. Although I had paid up for the pram and cot, I left it in the shop. This is because they say it is bad luck to have it in the house before the baby is born. I felt that I had more than my fair share of bad luck and I was not going to tempt fate! I was in hospital for about seven days and once I knew when I was going to be released, I asked Winston to call in the shop and ask them to deliver the pram and cot for our homecoming. I could not wait to get home and wheel baby out in his new pram! The reason for the pram being in the hall was because Winston could not get it up the two flights of stairs. But it was the best homecoming I could have had. The pram symbolized a new beginning. At that time I did not realize that there were no beginnings or endings, just a continuous circle!

We took baby upstairs and settled him in his new cot. I had only just sat down when I heard Agnes come in. She shouted up the stairs, "Beatrice, are you up there? Can you come down?" I ran downstairs, thinking she wanted to welcome me home and ask to see baby. How wrong could I be! She started to shout at me, "You can get that bloody pram out of my hall – and if you think I am going to have a screaming baby in the house, you better think again!" I sat on the bottom stair in that dingy, dirty hall and felt like crying. What had started off by being a near perfect day had been spoilt. How could I have been so besotted that I assumed everyone would be as happy as I was about baby? And then I started getting angry – Agnes had known I was pregnant and that there would be a baby soon. How dare she speak to me in that tone!

I went upstairs to tell Winston what had happened, expecting him to go downstairs and tell her off. However, he calmed me down and convinced me not to say anything or we could find ourselves out in the street. He said that he would just have to try and get the pram upstairs. I was really upset and worried that we might scratch the pram on the narrow stairs. I know this sounds silly, but in some strange way that pram was an important symbol! I was also concerned about how I was going to manage once Winston returned to Colchester. How on earth was I going to take the baby out? Fortunately I did not have to face this dilemma. So perhaps there was someone looking out for me after all.

Winston did not have to return to Colchester, he was released from his sentence and would now be stationed at Padgate. We decided to name the baby 'Paul'. Paul must have sensed how tense we were. After the scene with Agnes, I tried to keep Paul as quiet as possible. Can you imagine trying to stop a newborn baby from crying? It is like trying to stop the tide from coming in! In order to keep the crying down, I used to take Paul outside for as long as I could. You know babies must be able to sense an atmosphere, if there is one. However hard we tried, Paul cried most of the time. I now realize that he must have been colic, but, as a new mother, all that I knew was that this child would not stop crying!

Winston and I used to take it in turns, at night, walking the floor with Paul, just to stop him from crying. Until Paul was three months old, we did not know a full night's sleep. I was fortunate that at this time Winston was supportive and helped me out. God only knows how I would have coped otherwise. Every night when Paul cried, Agnes would bang on the ceiling and yell for us to get out of her house. She started picking on me for every small thing. I just do not know why she changed so suddenly and to this day wonder about it.

* * *

Betty and I met after about a fortnight. It seemed a little strange to be sitting in this tranquil surrounding and talking about what must have been very difficult times for her. She was also anxious about how her children would respond to the story. The hardest thing for her was if they rejected her. I could not give Betty any guarantees and I had to say this. It was hard but by writing her story she was undertaking a difficult and painful journey. We talked about this whilst we had a cup of tea. Once we finished tea, Betty was eager to continue with her story.

* * *

As I mentioned the last time, Winston was stationed at the RAF Camp in Padgate. He travelled from Manchester to Padgate every day. He would leave the house at about 7a.m. and would not get back home until 5.30 p.m. When he got home, he was often too tired to help. Anyway, this was my chance to prove what a good wife and mother I was.

During the day I put up with Agnes's temper and caustic remarks, whilst running around trying to keep Paul happy. In the evenings I had to keep both Winston and Paul happy. Sometimes I was worn to a frazzle and I just wished Winston could be like he was in the first three months of Paul's birth. The moment I had thoughts like these, I would quietly tell myself off for being so ungrateful – did I not have a beautiful son and a hard working husband? I would then be extra nice to Winston.

But there were days when no amount of telling myself off helped. I can remember one such day as clearly as if it were yesterday. If you remember I had told you that the bathroom was a flight of stairs down. In order to avoid Agnes I used to creep downstairs to the bathroom to get water to bath Paul. If she heard me going up and down the stairs she would shout at me for 'wasting' water. So some days I would fill the baby bath with water and make do with it for all my jobs. One day I was trying to creep downstairs carrying the bath water to empty it. Winston was upstairs having a snooze. As I was about to take my second, or was it third, well it doesn't matter. As I took one of the steps I must have lost my footing and slipped and fell, the water going all over the stairs and me. She came running up the stairs and shouted about the water coming through the ceiling and spoiling her wallpaper. What wallpaper? At the same time Winston came out of our room and also shouted at me, telling me to be more careful. Can you believe it? I couldn't – here I was sitting on the floor, soaked to my skin, unable to stand up, possibly hurt and these two people were telling

ME off! Where was their humanity? If I hadn't felt so sore I would have probably laughed hysterically. I guess this was the first time I could not excuse Winston and saw a side of him I did not like very much. I also knew that the time had come to move.

Whenever I was out with Paul, I looked in all the paper shop windows to see if there were any rooms to let. One day I was lucky to see an advert just being put in the shop window. The advert was for two rooms to let and the rent was only thirty shillings a week. I took the address and went home excited. I had decided that as soon as Winston came home I would give him his tea and leave him with Paul, whilst I went to look at the rooms. Before Winston could get through the door I told him. I was so excited and he tried to calm me down and told me not to build up my hopes. He agreed to look after Paul, so after giving Winston his tea, I dressed up and went out to find the address that was clutched in my hand.

When I found the address I was surprised to see that the house was much better than I expected and was decent looking. I am not sure as to why I was surprised, perhaps it was that I had become so used to crummy accommodation that I just did not expect better. Anyway, I knocked on the door and again felt that sense of nervousness in the pit of my stomach.

I stood there with my fingers tightly crossed mentally rehearsing what it was I would say when the door opened. I was also praying that the rooms had not been taken. And, oh my God, Winston; how was I going to describe him – do I say "Oh, by the way my husband is black" – or "my husband is coloured and is in the RAF" – people were often impressed if you were in government service. However, before I could settle for a response, the door opened.

The woman at the door was neatly dressed and looked pleasant. The surprise on my face must have showed because she asked me if I needed any help. I mentally cleared my head and said that I was interested in the rooms to let. Imagine my sense of relief when she invited me to enter and have a look at the rooms. This meant that they must still be available. Once inside she confirmed that the rooms were still available and showed me into two ground floor rooms. Imagine GROUND floor rooms – no trudging up endless stairs. I could hardly contain my excitement. I looked around the rooms and although empty they were clean and bright. She said that both rooms were available unfurnished for thirty shillings a week.

I simply could not believe my luck and quietly pinched my arm to see that I was not dreaming. I was not dreaming! I said that I was very interested in the rooms but felt she needed to know that my husband was a coloured man. Again she did not look concerned and said that she did not mind as long as we were no trouble. I assured her that we were good people and she said that we could move in whenever we wanted. Returning to Agnes' house I had to stop myself from running all the way. At last an escape from that hellhole and that nasty woman!

I could not wait to tell Winston the good news.

The next day I told Agnes that we would be moving out and that we were giving her a week's notice. She was not pleased but I really did not care! For some time now I had been paying money on a weekly basis to a local furniture shop in order to buy some dining room furniture. That day I went down to the shop and made arrangements for delivery to our new address. I had not paid up for the furniture but the owner agreed that I could continue to pay off the low balance.

That week went by quickly. I was so happy and excited and some days I just could not contain my excitement. I started planning in my head what I would do to make the place homely – where I would place Paul's cot ... my dreaming went on and on....

The day finally arrived for us to move. I got up that morning feeling light hearted and happy. A new beginning! I sorted out breakfast singing to myself, Winston telling me to calm down. I was just getting Paul ready when there was a knock at the door. Still singing to myself I went downstairs and opened the door. A man was standing on the step. As I was about to ask him what he wanted I noticed a furniture van parked behind him.

The man said that they had been to the address I had given them, but the lady of the house said that we were not moving in. I laughed and said, "Oh, there must be some mistake. I'll go over and sort it out now."

I rushed upstairs to put on my coat muttering to myself, "You can't trust anyone to do a job...", came down and asked them to wait whilst I went round to the house.

I got to the house slightly out of breath, and knocked on the door. When the woman answered the door I said, "Thank goodness you are in; there seems to be some kind of confusion. The furniture van which came round had our things in it – you remember me, Mrs. Jones?" I gave her a broad smile.

She did not return the smile and I then knew that there was something seriously wrong. What she said next knocked the bottom out of my world. She said, quite matter of fact, "There is no mistake, I have changed my mind. I have given the matter some thought, and I will not feel safe with a coloured man in the house. These people get up to all sorts of things and I run a respectable house. I have heard that they keep knives and I really cannot take a chance. So sorry!"

I couldn't believe what I was hearing and pleaded with her. "I have a baby and we have handed in our notice at our present accommodation, we have nowhere to go." She simply would not budge, repeating herself like a broken record. I even tried to say that we would only stay until we found somewhere else to live but she would not have it. I started crying, a mixture of feelings churning in my insides – anger, frustration and a deep sense of hurt. I told her that I couldn't understand why she hadn't contacted us to tell us that she had changed her mind. She said that she had had enough, and did not need to explain herself to me; before I could say anything she shut the door.

I felt an enormous rage welling in me and I could have kicked that door down but what purpose would that serve! I turned away thinking, 'what on earth am I going to do? Where were we going to go?' I knew that Agnes would take great pleasure in our predicament and would not allow us to stay.

You know in those days we had no way of challenging people's actions or attitudes. No Race Relations Act, nothing to protect us from such blatant discrimination. What was I to say to Winston?

I got back to the house and told the man to take the furniture back to the shop. I would come and settle things as soon as possible. Then I broke the news to Winston. I could see from the expression on his face that he was dying to say, 'I told you so'; instead he persuaded me to go and talk to Agnes. Much as I hated doing that I had no alternative – I had baby Paul to think about. Swallowing my pride I went downstairs to ask Agnes if we could stay. I told her that the rooms had fallen through, that we had nowhere to go and could she let us stay. I begged her; I was just short of getting on my bended knees, and she just smirked. That woman did not show us an ounce of pity and insisted that we had to leave that day. I pleaded to be allowed to remain at least for that night because of the baby – but she insisted that we left that night! There was no option but to leave. I had no time to rant and rave or give way to my feelings. Winston and I made some feeds up in a flask, packed our few belongings, wrapped Paul up warmly and left. We could not take the cot with us and told Agnes we would be back for it. We put Paul in the pram and set off walking towards Moss Side, which was known as 'Little Africa'.

Moss Side, Manchester.

Moss Side was the only likely place to find accommodation; it was the only area where people like us would be accepted. At that time there was no place like Homeless Families or Housing help and so we literally walked the streets that evening. I was so tired that I could have slept on a park bench but I had to think about Paul. You know he was a real angel and did not cry once! Isn't it strange? It was as if he knew that we had reached the end of our tether and that he needed to help by being good! We walked for most of that night until we found a room in St Bee Street.

The room was vile; it was bare without a stick of furniture and it smelt. We had little choice – either take it or be on the streets all night. So we took it! Once in the room we sat on the filthy floor and I desperately wondered how we could improvise for a bed. I then remembered a woman I had met in the hospital when I was having Paul – I had become quite friendly with her. I knew she lived in the area. I told Winston to keep an eye on Paul whilst I went to see if I could borrow a couple of chairs. Fortunately she agreed to lend me a couple of chairs. Can you imagine how weird I must have looked, carrying two chairs in the middle of the night? I prayed that the police would not come by. In fact that is why I went to see this friend instead of Winston; I did not want to take the risk of him being stopped by the police and possibly being arrested.

When I got to our room I was exhausted and my arms felt as if they were hanging from their sockets. My eyes felt like sandpaper and I did not have the energy to think of food. Winston and I slept on those hard backed chairs whilst Paul slept in his pram. The last thought as I dropped off was, "I will have to call at the furniture shop and ask them to deliver the items of furniture that I had been making payments on." That week was one of the most dreadful weeks I had ever had up to that point.

I remember that it was snowing. Yes, we were put out on the streets in the middle of winter. It was snowing that week, and the snow came in through a hole in the roof. The room was filthy but I could not clean it, as I had no fire to dry the place. There was a fireplace but we had no coal as it was still being rationed, although the war was over it would be a week before we could get our supply. I used to go to my friend's house (the one who lent us the chairs) and she would let me bathe Paul and make feeds for him, as we didn't have a cooker. I managed to keep our clothes clean by going to the old washhouse.

All this time Winston was still travelling to and from work; at least he used to get a hot meal in Camp!

Just when I thought this nightmare was never going to end, things started getting easier. They were still difficult but I guess as I established a routine it felt easier. In time we managed to get a bed and Paul, of course, had his cot. We got that from Agnes' house. When we eventually got some coal, I had a fire roaring. I scrubbed that room from top to bottom and that helped release a lot of my pent up anger. I was going to make this horrible room a home! If I sound like I am repeating myself, don't be surprised I often felt a sense of 'deja vu' and kept saying the same things to myself, in order to convince myself that I had some control over my destiny!

Once the floor was scrubbed I bought some lino to put down. We had also managed to pick up a second hand cooker. The coal had to be kept in a box in the room so I put up a curtain to separate the 'kitchen' area from the 'living ' area. The 'kitchen' area comprised of the coal box and the cooker! It was not exactly what I would describe as 'cosy' but it was comfortable.

We were the only married couple in the house all the other rooms were let as bed-sits with mainly women living in them.

* * *

Betty smiled wryly. "You would think that by now that I would be a little less naive, and, more worldly wise. I could not understand why the house was so quiet during the day and got noisy at night. Often in the early hours of the morning we would be woken up by lots of shouting and screaming, as if people were fighting. Winston also insisted that I was not to talk to any of the girls! And yet it did not click! Anyway I used to get lonely during the day, and became friendly with one of the women in the house. It was then I learnt that the girls were all prostitutes and the men they were with were their pimps. These men were living off them and if they didn't earn enough money, they would be beaten up."

Betty leaned back in her armchair and sighed. "Thinking back, I hated living in that horrible house. Do you know, the landlord had to cheek to tell me that I would have to take my turn cleaning the bathroom, as this was communally used? 'Take my turn!' The bathroom was in a disgusting state – it did not look as if it had ever been cleaned. There was a big hole under the bath and everyone used to throw empty bottles, tins and rubbish there; I am surprised that I never saw any rats. At night, the landlord would turn off the electricity so I often looked after Paul in the dark. I used to go to the clinic regularly, and the health visitor used to sometimes come to the house. She was concerned about the environment and promised to try and see if she could find us a better place. Yes, that was some rat-hole."

* * *

The worst of it was that Winston showed no real interest in finding somewhere else to live. I guess because he was away all day until the evening, he did not have to think about what Paul and I had to put up with. He just came home to eat and sleep. We hardly ever talked, even at Agnes's we managed to have a laugh. Now we were like two strangers sharing a room. I spent my day cleaning the room and caring for Paul, looking forward to the company of my tired and silent husband in the evening. The long winter days were depressing and lonely; I hated every minute spent in that house on St. Bee Street.

Things started getting worse between Winston and me. At least when we did not talk with each other I tried to explain it away as Winston being tired. He now had started coming home later and later. Some nights I got tired of waiting up and went to bed. The next morning I would find his evening meal in the bin. When I asked him why he was getting in so late; he said that he had to do extra duty. At first I believed him, but when it became almost every night, I became suspicious. I hated myself for doubting him, I believed as a wife I had to trust and have faith in my husband. Although I knew that he could not be doing so much extra duty I pushed my doubts to the back of my mind, as I did not want to be accused of nagging him.

The easy relationship between us had gone. We always seemed tense in each other's company. To make matters worse I found out that I was expecting another child. I guess at this time I did not feel terribly excited as my main worry was how I was going to bring up another child in this dump? This was no place for children. But Winston would not talk with me or discuss my worries. In fact he was quite irritated to find out that I was pregnant.

Time went by slowly, with Winston staying out later and later and not coming home some nights. I remember the first night he stayed out – I must have fallen asleep and got up about 4a.m. I realized that he was not home as his dinner was still in the oven. I panicked but did not know what to do. Who would be interested in a missing black man? I worried all that day and decided that if he did not return that night I would contact the RAF base. At around 7p.m. he sauntered in asking for his tea with no word of explanation. I tried to tell him how worried I had been but he just laughed at me. "Woman all you do is worry!" I shut up after that and the pattern was set. If he was back home late or had stayed out all night he stopped making excuses and I stopped asking for them.

During this time I still worked hard at keeping our room clean and looking after Paul. He was my solace. Whenever I felt low I would talk to Paul, of course he could not understand what I was saying, but his face was my delight. When he smiled or gurgled I felt a light go on inside of me. This was my child, and I was going to do the best for him.

As I started 'showing', and with Winston's lack of interest I an ashamed to say that I started to let myself go. I was always very conscious of my appearance and always tried to look nice. My outward appearance was the way I challenged the world. Now nothing seemed to matter and I lost interest in myself. I think that I had stopped being a person and had become a robot – carrying out my motherly and wifely duties mechanically.

* * *

I could see the despair and pain in Betty's eyes. A solitary tear trickled down her worn face and her voice virtually disappeared; I had to move nearer to hear what she said next. In a low voice she continued her story.

Winston's affair...

Sunday afternoon I decided to take Paul out for a walk. Winston was on duty and I was tired of being cooped up in that house. As I was out walking with Paul I saw this man who looked like Winston but who had a woman on his arm. I visibly shook my head and looked again – it *was* Winston.

At the same time that I acknowledged that it was Winston, I had to admit to myself that he was having an affair and had been unfaithful to me. It is far too painful to describe what I felt as I stood there transfixed, with this man's son. A little part inside of me, deep inside of me, slowly died. All I knew was that I had gone through hell for this man, I had given up everything to be with him, I was still going through hell living in that awful house and that with a click of his fingers he had deserted me. I felt completely alone. And I then heard Joe's voice telling me that I had made my bed and would have to lie on it. I went home feeling that someone had died. Paul demanded my attention and I did what I had to, and went to bed.

That night I did not sleep but my head kept whirring with one image after another of this woman and Winston. I heard him come in but I lay very still and pretended to be asleep. To this day I do not know whether Winston had also seen me that fateful day.

One night Winston came home in a foul mood. I was kneeling down tending the fire. I could not afford to keep it going all day so I often lit it an hour before Winston was due to come home. It wasn't that we did not have the money but he never gave me much money. What little he gave for housekeeping he sometimes took out of my purse again. As I was just about to put some more coal on the fire, he shouted, "That is enough coal!"

I said in what I thought was a reasonable tone, "Winston, if I don't back the fire up, it will go out." And then before I could move he came over to me and hit me with his fist right across the room. I couldn't believe it – Winston had never struck me before, even at our most difficult moments.

I lifted myself off the floor and yelled, "what was that for?" and went to strike him. I put all my weight behind that punch but I was no match for this 6-foot tall man. He seemed possessed and his face had the look of a mad man. I was terrified but somehow my brain had not got the message that things were out of control. He knocked me down again and again – I was like a rag doll. When I couldn't get up anymore he started kicking me. My ears were full of the sounds of my own screams and of my little boy crying. Yes, Paul was in the room when this happened. When it felt like he was not going to stop until he killed me, he suddenly stormed out of the room.

I dragged myself to my feet – it hurt me to breathe. It felt as if I was on automatic pilot. I was terrified that he would return and possibly kill me and I knew that for Paul and my safety I had to get out of that house. Where would I go? I had only one place – it was Joe's! I wrapped Paul up and crept out of the house.

* * *

As Betty talked I sensed coldness around her. She was telling this part of the story as if she was describing it happening to someone else. "I simply did not think about the state I was in. How I must have looked, all cut up and bruised. It was a three-bus journey to Joe's and I arrived at his front door in the early hours of the morning. You know I had not thought about what I was going to do if he turned me away. I somehow knew that once he saw me he would not reject me. I knocked on the door."

* * *

When Joe answered the door, the expression on his face said it all. He started to cry. "Girl, what has happened? What a mess you have made of your life." I did not need reminding; every bone in my body knew this. When I told him that I was scared about being at home because of Winston's rage, he said, "I am going to find him and kill him!" Ironic isn't it? It needed me to be in that state for my brother to react.

Anyway, we did not talk that night as Joe reckoned what I needed was a good night's sleep. When I got up the next day, Joe had gone to work and left a message with Josie that I should stay put until he returned.

I had something to eat, and washed and fed Paul and then decided that I was going back to try and sort things out. I believed it would be better if I tried to sort things out rather than have Joe involved. Now, when I look back I think this must have been the most stupid thing I did. Here I had the chance to cut my losses and run – my brother was one hundred per cent with me and I foolishly threw that away. I guess that if I had remained at Joe's the story would end now, or might be an altogether different tale. Who was it that said that we make our own destiny? Josie tried to persuade me to stay, at least until Joe returned. I had made my mind up and left, leaving Joe a short note thanking him for his support but saying that I was the only one who could deal with this mess.

When I got home, I let myself in the front door and went up to our room. I was shocked to see the door padlocked. I guessed it was Winston's way of stopping me from getting in. I broke the lock and went in. Winston had put photos of some woman all around the room I couldn't believe that he could be so callous – putting photos in a room that I had struggled to make our home! I was hurt but also furious and tore the photos into shreds. As soon as I did this, I knew that I was in danger of getting another beating but I did not care. At that moment I felt that I could have killed Winston and the woman too.

I waited and waited all that day and night but Winston did not come home. It was the next night that he returned. He was furious that I had broken into the room and torn up his photographs, and as he shouted my body tensed up for another beating. But I did not get the beating I was expecting! I left things as they were that night, as I did not want to get him worked up unnecessarily.

The next day, and the next, and the next… I wanted us to talk and to try and sort things out. Winston wasn't interested; he just ignored me and carried on as before acting as if my bruised face did not exist. He went out when he wanted to and stayed out as he pleased. I never knew from one day to the next, where I was with him, whether he would be back home or what kind of mood he was in. This uncertainty and tension was affecting me and Paul, and I finally decided that I needed to take control of the situation. What did I decide to do? I decided we would move. I actually convinced myself that it would help if we could find a better place to live. This place was getting us both down and it was not fit for children. Also with the second baby due in a few months it would be better if we moved.

I started to look hard for a place. I heard of two rooms going in Russell Street, just off Princess Road. It was near Moss Side. The house from the outside seemed in a nice condition. The rooms were heaps better than any of the ones we had been in. The thought of having a bedroom, as well as a sitting room, really appealed to me. It would be great to be able to put the children to bed and have some separate space and time for ourselves to us. Winston agreed to move. I felt that things were going to change, with more space to be together, this was going to solve all our marital problems.

I have always held myself responsible for things going wrong in our marriage. I blamed myself and felt that I was doing something wrong. Although I never could work out what it was that I was doing wrong, I felt that I would need to work harder at getting things right and pleasing my husband.

A new start, my second child on the way ...

One wet weekend we moved to our new home. I worked hard at making it a home and managed to make it quite cosy. However, things did not get any better between Winston and I. He carried on as before so I spent long lonely evenings in that living room, whilst Paul slept in the other room. For some reason my ability to bounce back was non-existent. I started to worry more and more. A second child was due soon, Winston simply did not care, and I hardly had enough money to feed Paul. Winston would think nothing of taking the last shilling from my purse. I tried hiding my purse but he always found it, or threatened me until I gave him the money. I was forever going to the corner shop to ask them to let me have bread and milk on the 'tic'. Whilst I begged in order to feed his child he would be spending money on his fancy woman! However I would do anything for Paul – he was my child too – in fact more mine than Winston's! This way I at least managed to ensure that Paul was fed, but I was hardly eating myself and was getting very thin in spite of being heavily pregnant.

Most of the time I was like a zombie - I acted as if I were on some kind of drug. My whole life revolved around Paul - I had lost all interest in rescuing my marriage and in myself. My apathy seemed to go on forever. As he had promised, a couple of weeks after moving into Russell Street, Joe came to see Winston and me.

Joe was shocked when he saw me and commented on my weight loss. He sat both Winston and me down and warned Winston not to hit me again. His eyes looked pained when he told me to look after myself and that he was worried that if I kept neglecting myself, I would not live through the birth of my second child. I could not tell him that I really did not care – to drop dead would be an end to this misery – and I was only carrying on for my boy's sake. Who would look after him if anything happened to me? Not Winston!

I smiled at Joe and sent him on his way with reassurances that I would be okay. I had decided to have the baby at home as I had no one to look after Paul. I did not feel able to trust Winston with Paul. The midwife was booked but I still had no idea as to who would look after me while I was in bed. Winston was never home and I had no expectations that he would make time to look after me. I lived a day at a time, that is if you could call it 'living' – my mind could no longer cope with thinking beyond the day. All I knew was that 'I had made my bed...'.

You know sometimes people say that 'God works in mysterious ways.' I am not religious or have any deep belief in 'God' but what happened next makes me feel that there may be a lot of truth in the saying. In fact, come to think of it whenever I felt that I had reached the pits of despair, something happened. I am sure that someone has always been there to help me through my worst moments. That someone was there then. A week before the baby was due, Winston...

* * *

At this point I lost my concentration and Betty's voice faded away. I looked at the woman sitting across from me and thought of all the women survivors of violence that I had worked with. Her story could be any one of theirs – the recriminations, the blame, every small coincidence blazing into a flame of hope. Always, 'it was my fault. If only I did things differently.' A part of me wanted to shake Betty and say, 'It was not your fault. You cannot hold yourself responsible for your husband's behaviour. He is the one responsible!' But I knew these would only be words with little meaning. Betty had spent a lifetime blaming herself and it was not going to change just because I wished it to. The sense of powerlessness, which came over me, was reflected in Betty. I could understand her sense of hopelessness and futility. I shook my head when I realized that I had stopped listening to Betty.

I prompted her, "Betty, what was that you were saying about Winston?"

"Winston came down with chicken pox a week before the baby was born. If things were not so desperate it would have been something to laugh about. Of all the coincidences!" She started to laugh. "He had spots all over his face and couldn't shave. I guess this stopped him from seeing his woman friend. Winston always had to be immaculately turned out. He was well and truly stuck at home with me and I had got an unexpected minder!"

A week later at 4a.m. Betty went into labour.

* * *

It was in the very early hours of the morning, must have been around 3a.m., that I started getting bad cramps. I knew that the baby was coming.

Normally Winston would not have been in, but because of his chicken pox he was in bed beside me. I woke him up and told him to go and get the midwife and I would try and light the fire. My pains were so bad that I had to abandon lighting the fire and lay down breathing deeply. I was trying not to panic. With Paul I had been in labour for several hours, but with this one it felt like it was going to be a quick birth.

After what felt like hours, although it couldn't have been, the midwife arrived with Winston panting at her side. From the time the midwife walked through the front door, she never stopped complaining. She moaned because Winston had chicken pox, that she shouldn't have been the one attending me, and questioned why I hadn't lit the fire. I ignored her and concentrated on my breathing, as the pain was intense.

At 5.30 a.m. my second child was born and he was a boy. My baby was so beautiful; a chubby, little baby with tiny black curls clustered on his head. Looking at that innocent child you would not have thought about the trauma he must have experienced when I was carrying him.

I decided to call him Crispin. This should have been a happy time for me, but, as I cradled little Cris in my arms, I felt very lonely and very sad. I had thought that since Winston was around he would be of some help. More fool I! He was a real swine and made it clear that I should not expect anything from him and that he intended to do as little as possible for me. When I needed a drink, I had to get up and make it myself. When Cris's nappies needed washing – we didn't have disposables in those days – he brought me a bucket of water and some soap and left it by my bed. I had difficulty sitting up and so I would have to lean out of bed and wash the baby's things as best as I could using a bar of soap. No soapsuds to make things easier!

After a few days I started feeling stronger so it was easier for me to potter around. One of the first things I needed to do as soon as I was well enough to go out was to buy a pram. What happened to Paul's pram? Winston had it sold it without consulting me and had pocketed the money. At the time I didn't have the energy to have an argument about it. Now I wish I had. Even though I had been desperately short of money, I had been saving up my maternity allowance to use as a deposit for a pram. This was the only way I was going to be able to afford to get a pram, which I knew would be vital for taking the baby out. On my first day out, I went to the Post Office to draw the money out for this pram. I took the Post Office book out of my bag and opened it to sign the necessary pages. I was just about to sign and had to blink – I couldn't believe my eyes. All the money had gone – every last penny had been drawn out. The only person who could have done this was Winston. I left the Post Office in a daze and when I got home, burst into tears. I cried uncontrollably as if every last ounce of life was being drained out of me. How could he? How could Winston deprive his own son? How was I going to manage with a baby and a toddler? If I had to spend all my time indoors I would crack up. A prisoner in my own home!

Winston just explodes...

I had had enough! I decided to have it out with him that evening. He did not come home until late that night. He stank of drink but I was determined to challenge him for stealing that money. As soon as he sat down in the living room I asked him about the money and what he had spent it on. He just looked at me and his eyes seemed to change colour and he exploded with temper. His fists were raised and I saw them too late as he rained blows on me. I fell to the floor and he started kicking me. In the sheer pain that I felt I wondered how he could do this to a defenseless woman. And suddenly the woman at the camp – the one who had accused him of stealing from her – her face flashed before my eyes. Why? I don't know why.

While these images flashed through my mind strange sounds were coming from my mouth. I realized that I was screaming. My screams did not stop him and I felt as if my face had been split open. Just as suddenly as he had started hitting me, he stopped and left me on the floor. He went into the bedroom and went to sleep! Looking at him sleeping I could have killed him for I knew that when he got up, he was likely to start all over again. I did not allow myself to think rationally. I bundled a few baby clothes and some food into a bag and picked Cris up.

Paul was asleep and I did not dare try to wake him up, as it would have aroused Winston. I decided that I would have to leave him with Winston and just take Cris. I really do not know how I could have left Paul behind – my only excuse is that in the state I was, it seemed the only sensible thing to do. Also I was not sure how I would manage two children without a pram. I convinced myself that Winston would not dare hurt Paul and would look after him. How stupid could I get? Anyway I left the house as I was desperate to get away and made my way to the only person who would help me.

I got the all night bus to Stockport making my way to Joe's. People stared at me and the bus driver asked, "Are you okay, love?" I must have looked a dreadful sight, my eyes were nearly closed, what felt like dry blood was caked on one side of my face, and my nose still trickled with blood.

When I finally got to Joe's, it must have been about one in the morning. They were in bed when I knocked on the front door. I was almost giving up hope of having them answer the door, when I heard footsteps. Joe opened the door and at the sight of me, he said, "Betty, love, have you been in some kind of an accident?" Was history repeating itself?

It felt as if someone had pushed a button for 'Action Replay'. It was just like before – Joe crying and threatening to kill Winston, Josie helping me to clean up my face, me settling the baby, only it was Cris this time and not Paul, trying to get sleep that night, Joe asking for Paul and telling me to wait until he returned from work the next day and he would take me back to the house...

It was kind of Josie and Joe to let me stay but the next morning I started to worry about Paul. Part of me felt sure that Winston would ring up the Camp the next day and ask for a day off. He was good at making excuses and he was bound to do so in order to look after Paul. The other half clearly said that I could not trust Winston. I had visions of him disappearing with Paul and never being able to see my baby again. Joe had made it clear that I had a home with him as long as I needed it. He would accompany me back so that I could get Paul and our belongings and leave Winston on his own. I waited until lunchtime that day, steadily getting more and more worried about Paul. When it felt as if my head would burst I told Josie that I would have to go back and could not wait for Joe.

Josie tried to persuade me to wait, reminding me how dangerous Winston was. By now my sanity had returned and I was furious with myself. What kind of mother was I? How could I have left Paul with someone like Winston? What was I thinking? As these thoughts raced through my head I was deaf to my sister-in-law's pleas. I got Cris ready and tried to reassure Josie that I would be all right. The only way she let me through that door was by promising her that I would first go to the local police station and ask for a policeman to accompany me home. I promised and left making the long journey home. When I got to Moss Side I had every intention of going to the police station and at the last minute decided otherwise, thinking it would be quicker to go home directly.

As I neared the house I saw a man standing near the front door and wondered what he was up to. Approaching the front door, he came up to me and said that he was a plain-clothes officer and he wanted to talk to me. I wondered why he wanted to talk to me but at the same time felt relieved that I would not have to enter the house and face Winston on my own. When we were in the house there was no sign of Paul or Winston. 'Oh! God something has happened to Paul that is why this man is here' flashed across my mind.

I turned to the man, by this time another man had joined him, and said in a panic, "What has happened to my son? Where is Paul?"

The man was looking at me in a strange way, as if I smelt or had crawled from under a stone. He said very coldly, "Your child is with your next door neighbours!"

I was puzzled." My next door neighbours? Why, where was my husband?"

"At his work, of course, where did you expect him to be? We have contacted the Camp and your husband should be on his way home. Forget your husband, we would like to know why you left your child in the house on his own?" Forget my husband, how could I? I didn't leave the child on his own, I left him with my husband.

They did not look as if they believed me. I explained to them what had happened the night before; that I had run away to my brother's fearful for my safety. I had left Paul behind, as he was asleep. Winston was in the house at the time also asleep and I was just returning from my brother's. At that point Winston walked in and I was left not knowing whether they believed me. They asked me to leave the room, as they wanted to speak to Winston alone. After what felt like hours, but in fact must have been about 15 minutes, they asked me to join them. I could not believe what they were saying. I thought I knew the worst of Winston but this was bad; he had lied to them. He had told them that I was in the house that morning when he had left to go to work; that we had a bit of an argument the night before but he had thought that we had sorted our differences. He thought I must have left Paul on his own to get back at him. And they seemed to believe his stupid story.

I asked them to look at my face – did it look as if we had 'a bit of an argument?' Winston had beaten me up badly and I had gone to my brother's; they could check with Joe. But they seemed to have lost all interest and left warning me that if I were ever to leave my children on their own I would be imprisoned and the children would be put in a home! When they left I did not know whether to laugh or cry. Winston just leered at me and I felt as if he had physically beaten me up.

I later found out that the C.O. had asked Winston why had the police wanted him at home and Winston had said, "My wife has just had a baby and is suffering from depression. She went out and left the children on their own." I would not be surprised if this is what he told the neighbours too. It felt as if everyone believed Winston and no one believed me. The bruises on my body and face were ignored.

Many of the neighbours gave me dirty looks and avoided talking to me. I guess besides marrying a black man, they could now treat me like rubbish because I was seen as an 'uncaring' mother. The hardest thing was that they did not need to condemn me; I was the hardest judge of all. I blamed myself and kept mentally punishing myself. Perhaps that is why I remained with Winston. I had convinced myself that I did not deserve better – I was never going to win – and that I was going to have to make the best of whatever life held for me.

The swelling on my face got worse and it was painful to even smile. I had to go and see the doctor who referred me to the hospital. I had fractured a cheekbone and needed treatment. The doctor tried to advise me to leave Winston; Joe made contact with me and also begged me to leave Winston.

My mind had been made up. I told Joe that I was not going to leave Winston and that whether it sounds crazy or not, I still wanted to save my marriage. Joe could not understand my decision and I guess many people would also find it difficult. I did not understand it myself! How could I remain with a violent man? Someone who would probably kill me one day! All I knew was that I was very much on my own and I had two children to look after and they needed a family not just a mother. Once I made that decision I knew that I had forever shut Joe out, I could not hope to ever expect him to help me in the future.

It was at this point in my life I really missed my mother. If only she were still alive, she would have told me what to do from a woman's point of view. Both my parents were dead and I missed my mother most. She had died when I was a child but I still had memories of this loving woman. I wanted my children to have the same memories of me. In the eyes of the world they would never be white, and I did not want to be blamed for depriving them from the knowledge of their black father.

And so, although I had a chance to leave Winston and make a fresh start, I remained with the man, determined to make a life for my children and myself. My first priority was to get a job, as I did not want to be financially dependent on Winston. I found a job cleaning at Withington Hospital and a woman who would mind

Paul and Cris for 30 shillings a week. This would not leave me with much but it was better than having no money at all, or having to beg Winston for a few shillings. Someone had given me an old pram so I was able to push the children round to the baby sitter every day. The woman's name was Mary. She was married to a West Indian and had three children. Her house was clean and her children were always tidy and happy looking. I hoped she would look after Paul and Cris like her own but at least on one score I was reassured. I knew that she would not pick on them because of their colour.

Mary had let one of the rooms in her house to another woman called Louise. Louise was also married to a West Indian and had three boys. She was Jewish and had been disowned by her parents and family because of her relationship with a black man. We all had a lot in common as they were also having a rough time with their husbands. The three of us struck up a kind of friendship and at least I no longer felt so completely alone.

Once I started work my day began at 6a.m. I had to get the children fed, washed and dressed. The next thing was dropping them off at Mary's house. I always took some baby food and enough nappies for the day. It was hard work pushing that old pram with two children in it. After dropping the children off I made my way to work. Work began at 8a.m. and ended at 4.30 p.m. Straight after work I would go and collect the children and make my way home.

Every alternate day I would go to the washhouse to wash the children's clothes. On these days Mary offered to look after the children but as I could not afford to pay her, I instead took her washing and did it with mine. Some days I felt so weary that I just did not want to continue, but the taste of my relative independence kept me going. Things between Winston and I did not get any better, but now at least he now left me alone.

One day whilst I was sorting out the clothes to take to the washhouse, I was checking through Winston's trouser pockets. I always did this as a matter of routine. This time I found a piece of paper with a woman's name and telephone number. I also found a couple of tickets for a holiday in Bournemouth. I hid the tickets amongst my underwear and decided to ring the number on the slip of paper. I was sure this must be the woman Winston was having an affair with.

I rang the number and a woman came to the phone. I asked to speak to 'Jessie' as that was the name on the paper. The woman asked me to hold on and I heard her shout, "Jessie, there is someone on the phone for you." I could hear a lot of background noise – laughter, talking and clinking of glasses. I guessed that Jessie worked in a pub. Much later I found out that I was right. She must have come over to the phone thinking I was a friend and I heard this friendly 'hello'.

I said, "You do not know me but you know my husband. I am Mrs. Jones, Winston's wife."

At this she said that she was very busy and was going to put the phone down.

"If you put the phone down, I know where you work. I shall come there and show you up." Of course I was bluffing but she wasn't to know that. She did not put the phone down but made it clear she had nothing to say to me.

"You might not want to talk to me but I need to talk to you. I can do this at your workplace or you could come to my house.

The choice is yours, but I am deadly serious when I say that I want to talk to you." My tone of voice seemed to convince her and she agreed to come over one evening after work.

Although I had only one decent frock I dressed myself up as if waiting to go into battle. In some ironic way I guess I was doing just that. When she turned up I was surprised to see that she was an older woman. She must have been in her late forties. I had expected to see someone younger or around my own age. I was only twenty-three at the time.

I must have had a smile on my face and she asked me what was I smiling at? Trying to suppress a hysterical laugh I apologized if I seemed rude and said that I was surprised to find out that my husband's mistress was an older woman. I then asked her if she knew that Winston had two little children and because he was spending all his money on her he was leaving us to starve.

At first she did not want to believe me but when I took her into the bedroom and showed her Paul and Cris asleep, she looked shocked. She admitted that she had not known Winston was married with two little children and promised me that she would not see him any more. Oh! How desperately I wanted to believe her.

After she left I took the holiday tickets from amongst my underwear and left them on the table. I felt I did not have to worry about Winston going away on holiday with this woman as she had promised me that she would end the relationship. A week later the tickets were missing. The holiday had been arranged for the first week in June. It was the second day in June and I knew with certainty that Winston had taken those tickets and would be at the bus station waiting to go away. In all the time that the tickets had remained on the table we both acted as if they were invisible. He proffered no explanations and I asked no questions. My sixth sense also said that the relationship with Jessie had not ended. If it had I was expecting to be beaten up for daring to see her. So when the tickets went missing I just knew that they were going away together.

A cold rage seemed to engulf me. I dressed myself up and put on the one shabby coat I had, got Paul and Cris ready, put some food and nappies in a bag, loaded all this and the two children in the pram and made my way to the bus station. When I got to the bus station it was very busy. People jostled me; everyone seemed to be impatient, waiting to go away. I had to keep an eye on Paul, as I was scared that he would topple out of the pram. He was getting a little too big for that old pram.

As I looked around frantically, I had just started berating myself for being so suspicious when I saw Winston. He was on the platform where the Bournemouth bus was due in. Dressed to kill! The woman with him was Jessie – she looked very attractive in a beautiful coat with her immaculately done up hair and made up face. I felt dowdy and nearly turned away. And then my anger took over and before I could let reason take over I found myself standing next to them.

I must have taken the children out of the pram because I remember holding Cris in my arms and Paul was holding the hem of my coat. I have no memory of what I said but as if in slow motion I saw my fist being raised and flying across Jessie's face. Her nose started to bleed and Winston looked about ready to strike me.

By this time a crowd had gathered. As if in a dream I heard someone shouting, "Fight! Fight! Two women are beating each other up!"

The crowd of people around us grew larger and people must have guessed as to what was going on. A woman standing next to me said, "Give me your baby love, and go give her a good hiding."

Why was I hitting Jessie when it was Winston who was the bad one, the one who was hurting me? Paul was crying out aloud, obviously frightened, whilst Cris whimpered in my arms. All the fight drained out of me and I started shaking. Someone must have taken me over to the Cafe and bought me a cup of tea.

The next thing I became aware of was a man bending over me saying he needed to talk to me to find out what was going on. Somebody had obviously called the 'cruelty man'! In a voice which did not sound like mine, I explained that my husband was swanning away on holiday with another woman leaving me with his two children with no money to feed them.

The man went to talk to Winston and I knew that Winston would once again spin some story, which this officer would swallow. Whilst the man was talking to Winston I saw the bus leave and Jessie was on it.

After some time the Cruelty Officer came over and explained that Winston had agreed not to go away and if I went home he would follow me. I was too upset to say anything and made my way home. I went home and waited and waited. My husband did not come home that day. He had taken the next bus and gone to Bournemouth!

Two weeks later Winston returned from his holiday, looking fit and relaxed. I, on the other hand, looked twice my age; tired and worn out. He acted as if nothing had happened. We had developed a way of distancing ourselves from each other. He did not volunteer any explanations and I did not ask. In some ways I was relieved that he had returned in a good mood, as I had been bracing myself for a good hiding.

I was still working at the hospital struggling to make ends meet. I might as well have been on my own, given that I never saw the colour of Winston's wages. You know he was so arrogant. On his return he had the cheek to tell me that he had spent all his wages on the holiday, he still had a week of holiday left and he had no money. Typically I ended up having to feed him as well as the children and myself and paying the rent for that period. All this had to come out of the balance of my wages after tax and paying Mary for looking after the children.

During the week he was at home Winston demonstrated over and over again just how thoughtless he really was. Not once did he say, "Betty, you look tired. Can I do anything to help? Perhaps drop the children off?" This was my fantasy – that the man I had given up everything for showed me some compassion. I did not want or expect anything else. But that was a dream.

The reality was that I was working my fingers to the bone trying to manage on my meager earnings, very often not eating properly so that I could feed my husband and children.

* * *

Betty sighed and looked at me. Perhaps she saw the question in my eyes. "Why did I just not leave him? I have asked myself the question a thousand times. I know that I sound such a drag and you must be wondering where is the woman who loved dancing and having a good time? That side of me had been worn down by constant worry.

Despite the fact that my life was not very funny, I did have a sense of humour."

Betty began to laugh. "I remember when the coal man used to come, he would shout up the stairs to see if anyone wanted coal. The man who had the room opposite us was a West Indian and was called 'Titus'. The coal man could not pronounce his name and would shout up to him, 'Tight Arse, do you want some coal?' We would be in stitches and I used to laugh until my sides hurt. However as the days went by there seemed less and less to laugh about – but life went on."

We both had a good giggle at the incident and that seemed to relieve some of the tension which had been building up in the front room.

Betty continued.

* * *

After that week Winston was back to work and things did not change. Late nights, not coming home at nights, me struggling with the children on a day-to-day basis. My life was work and bed, day in and day out. I did not know what leisure was. Many a time Mary would invite me for an evening out, but I could not go, as I had no one to look after the children. Paul and Cris were the centre of my world but at times of deep despair I sometimes resented them. Much as I loved them, and I loved them dearly, I sometimes wondered what my life would have been if they were not around. I wondered if my relationship with Winston would have been better. Perhaps he resented the children? I would then get very angry at my thoughts and would look at Paul and Cris and be thankful for them. They were my lifeblood.

One Sunday whilst I was seeing to Cris, Paul went missing. I had a gate at the top of the stairs to stop Paul from falling downstairs and somebody had left the gate open. I made sure that Cris was safe on the bed and ran outside onto the main road. Paul was looking in the shop windows across the road. He had crossed the busy main road on hi s own! Running across the road I grabbed him. I was petrified and did not know whether to shake or hug him. He could have been killed.

Paul and I returned to the safety of our rooms and I felt a boiling anger at Winston. It was one thing if he did not want to be bothered by us but he could at least find us a decent place to live - somewhere with a bit of garden for Paul to play in. That evening I told Winston what had happened. It was one of the few evenings he was at home. He also seemed in a jovial mood so I decided to take the opportunity. I pleaded with him to go and talk to his C.O. at Camp and see if we could get married quarters. Accommodation worked on a point system and we were already on the waiting list, but way down.

Winston had a way with words and I pandered to his vanity and convinced him that he could tell them that our circumstances had altered and the children were getting bigger and difficult to manage in our rented accommodation. Winston magnanimously agreed to talk to the C.O. So you see I was learning!

Weeks later Winston came home with a big grin on his face. I thought he might have won the pools or something along those lines. He told me that the C.O. had called him into his office and told him that he was trying to get us a property with R.A.F. Hiring. It seemed that they had a house that they rented from some private individual and they used it as married quarters. The house had been let to an officer and his family and they were now leaving but the lease of the house was still running. Given our circumstances and the fact that there was no accommodation in R.A.F. Padgate he thought that he could make arrangements for us to have it. This sounded so wonderful that I did not know whether to believe Winston but I kept my fingers tightly crossed.

A couple of weeks later, we were told that we could move. We went to see the house, which was in Swinton. It would still involve Winston travelling to and from work but the distance involved was shorter. It was three-bedroom house with a large garden at the back. There was even some furniture in it. I was so excited and thrilled to bits. The children and I would be living in this lovely big house. Paul could play in the back garden and I would not have to worry about rent because the R.A.F. would deduct it from Winston's wages directly. As we looked around that house I felt as if I were a young bride waiting to move into her first home. This is how it should have been. Winston said that he had not seen me so excited for a long time and seemed contented to ride along with my enthusiasm. Deep inside me I felt that this was the answer to our marriage problems - a nice house in a nice neighborhood and no more pressure on me to go out to work, another new beginning? Things between Winston and me improved considerably. We were able to have some kind of a relationship.

He still stayed out some nights and I stopped trying to imagine whom he might be with. Life was a lot better and I was grateful for small mercies! Winston still kept me with very little money but I only felt relieved that he was treating me with some kindness. I was able to really enjoy the children.

I remember how naughty Paul was. He loved being in the garden and I had planted some bulbs, to make the garden look pretty. No sooner had I planted the bulbs he dug them out. I gave up trying to plant any flowers – he would only pull them out. On one occasion when my back was turned he set fire to the armchair. All I can say was, "Thank God that I was there at the time!" Once he locked me out of the house and I had to get the man next door to break open the door. He really did keep me on my toes. I had to watch his every move. If Paul was quiet you could be assured that he was up to something naughty.

Cris was very different. He was a quieter child, often content with his own company. It was a long time since I had felt so relaxed and happy. The laughter, which had been almost beaten out of me, could be heard around the house! Every time I discovered something new that Paul or Cris had achieved, moving from bedroom to bedroom, or just sitting in the garden. These were all little pleasures that I learnt to cherish. And then I found out that I was pregnant.

* * *

When Betty said that she was pregnant, she must have seen the surprise on my face. I had just assumed that Betty and Winston did not have any kind of a sexual relationship – so much for my awareness.

Betty laughed when she saw the expression on my face. "Yes, Winston and I did continue having sex even when I knew he was seeing other women. Sometimes it was against my will and sometimes not. I guess it was one of my wifely duties that I felt I needed to meet if I was going to save my marriage."

* * *

Anyway this was the first pregnancy I enjoyed. I had time to savour all the changes in my body and to wonder at the life growing inside of me. As I got nearer to the date of delivery Winston was given leave to be with me. History repeated itself : instead of spending time with me he started staying out very late. Perhaps he felt that since he did not have to go to work the next day he could burn the candle at both ends. Anyway, I had given up speculating about his behaviour, as long as he treated me with some respect, I was not bothered. One night he came home very late. I was in bed but could hear him being sick in the bathroom.

I got up to see if he was all right and found that he had been sick all over the house. I couldn't leave the house in that state, as I did not want Paul or Cris slipping in that muck. So in the early hours of the morning, 9 months pregnant, I had to scrub all the floors with detergent. It made me feel sick and I knew that I was in no fit state to be on my knees scrubbing floors but I had no choice.

The next day Winston did not even apologise for his mess, but went out and stayed out all night. That night, at about midnight I went into labour. I had not been feeling well all that day and thought it was probably cleaning the floors which had upset me. That night I couldn't sleep and was in a lot of pain. However I was sure the baby was not due yet and I did not want to call the midwife in too early. My memories of the last midwife advised me to be cautious. I also did not know the neighbours well and did not want to bother people unnecessarily. Winston would be home soon so I tried to keep myself busy so as to stop thinking of the pain.

In order to keep myself occupied I set the table for breakfast for the children and sorted out some clean clothes for them. I then cleaned the house right through again. It was getting dark and I suspected that Winston would not be home that night. I was so terrified of being on my own when labour started that I decided to go down to the phone booth at the bottom of the road. The pain was increasing and I don't know how I made it to the phone! I phoned the midwife and the first thing she asked me was what was I doing out! Where was my husband? I felt like saying, "With some other woman!" but bit my tongue and asked her to come quickly. I had left the children asleep at home and wanted to get back just in case they should awake.

The midwife was very good and told me to go back home and make myself comfortable and she would come right away. With a sigh of relief I got home and had a bath and waited for the midwife. Whilst lying on the bed, I started worrying and the more worried I got the more agonizing the pain was. The midwife came and tried to calm me down. I was getting frantic. How could I trust Winston with the children? But, if not Winston who would look after them? Paul was a real handful and needed a watchful eye. Oh! God! I was once again on my own!

At 9.20a.m. my little girl was born. Instead of it being a straightforward birth I started to haemorrhage. Every thing had a dream-like quality about it. The only thing which was not dreamlike, was the intense pain in my insides. It was as if someone had a blowtorch and was burning me piece by piece. I remember the nurse rushing outside and I could hear her shout for my neighbours to phone the doctor and ask for an ambulance. There were people running in and out of the house – they were putting bricks at the bottom of the bed so as to lift up my legs to try and stop the bleeding.

The ambulance came. In those days it was called the 'Flying Squad'. I knew that I was very ill. The doctor gave me a blood transfusion and I thought that I was dying. I prayed to God frantically, "Please let me live – think of my children. You gave me beautiful children; please do not leave them without their mother." Tears must have flowed from my eyes because I could feel dampness on my face.

It must have been around this time that Winston came home. All I know is what I was told later. It seemed that he sat on the stairs crying, "I love you, please do not leave me. I don't want you to die." How I had longed to hear those words. But, now it mattered not one iota.

The doctor must have told him to pull himself together and that it was too late for regrets. He could make himself useful by looking after his two young children! At some point I must have been rushed into hospital because the next day I found myself in a hospital bed at Hope Hospital. Later that evening the doctor told me that Winston was waiting to see me. He reassured me that if I did not want to see him he could send him away. I was tired but I knew that I was going to have to see him at some point. I also wanted news of Paul and Cris.

When Winston approached the bed he started crying. Who was he crying for? I had shed too many tears – real tears – and this man was not going to break me! He started to plead for my forgiveness, saying he was sorry and that he would try and be a good husband to me. How many times had I heard the same thing? I forgave him and he would then start hurting and humiliating me all over again.

I was sick of his 'sorry' and I cut him short. "Where are the children? I hope you have not left them on their own?" He said that they were fine and that a neighbour was looking after them so that he could visit me in hospital.

He tried to talk with me but I was tired and I asked him to leave so that I could get some sleep. It was about nineteen days before I started feeling better. In all this time I did not see my baby very much as they kept her in the nursery. I longed to cradle her in my arms but knew that I was not strong enough as yet. The doctors and nurses were really caring and wonderful to me. For the first time in years, I felt cared for and cosseted.

I was in hospital for a considerable time and when I was ready to be discharged I looked a shadow of my former self. I had lost weight and was still very weak. I tired quickly and told the doctor that I was worried as to how I was going to cope on my own, as Winston was not much help. The doctor was really good and arranged for me to have a home help a couple of times a week.

On my return home Winston tried to convince me that he had changed. He stayed home a lot of the time but bitter experience told me this would not last. And I was right. My baby girl was born in June we called her Adele; she was a beautiful child with the most gorgeous eyes. Every time you looked at her you felt you were swimming in their glow. As if it were yesterday, I remember Christmas of that year. The Christmas of 1953!

Since returning home I had been saving a few shillings each week so that I could buy the children some small Christmas presents. A week before Christmas I put up a small tree and Paul helped me decorate it. It was hard for me to go into town so I asked Winston to get the children's presents. I gave him the money I had saved. That night he did not come home until the early hours of the morning. I was waiting up for him, as I was worried as to why he had not returned. He told me that he had spent all the money I had given him – not on presents for the children but on himself! I wept!

He then went to bed while I spent the rest of the time worrying about what I could give the children. We never spoke of the money again but I hoped that Winston would feel sorry and borrow some money and get some gifts for his children. That did not happen. He could not understand why I was making such a fuss! I had nearly lost my life – it was hardly surprising that I had wanted to make this a special Christmas! Christmas Eve arrived and I still had no presents. I put the children to bed and stared at the empty Christmas tree. Winston was not home and I felt as if I would burst.

The bitter tears flowed down my cheeks and as I tried to check them they flowed even faster. As my body shook with sobs there was a knock at the front door. I wiped my face and went to see who it was. It was the Vicar from the nearby church. I did not know what he was doing at my front door but I knew that my prayers had been answered. Inviting him in, he asked me why I was upset. I told him the whole pitiful story, too angry to try and protect Winston. After comforting me he left, only to return a short while later. He returned with presents for all the children! God had heard my prayers! Moments like these inspired me to hang on and to believe in the goodness of human beings.

In my darkest moments there was always a light. Life continued very much in the way it had for the past few years. The rent in the property where we were living had been put up and the R.A.F. told us we would need to move. I was worried about this as Winston had been put on a preliminary warning list and would not be offered a place to live. However it would seem that luck was on our side and we were offered married quarters in Padgate. This was probably around about when Adele was about three months old. I was relieved, as I was worried about how we were going to manage with three children and no roof over our heads. At long last we had got accommodation which was local to Winston's work.

This would mean that he could no longer blame the travelling for not coming home on time. Hopefully he would be around to help me a lot more.

We moved in on a Monday and on Wednesday, Winston came home to tell me that his posting for overseas had come through. He was going to be posted somewhere in the Middle East and was expected to leave on Friday.

I was stunned! We had not even unpacked, I did not know a soul on the camp and I was still recovering from my traumatic experience at the baby's birth. Winston was so excited. He was like a child with a new toy. Part of me wanted to yell, "What about me? How am I going to manage?" But I decided not to spoil things for him. And so I kept my mouth shut and allowed all my anxiety to build up inside of me.

Friday came too quickly. On Monday I had moved into our new house with my husband and children and on Friday I was still in this strange house but without my husband. Winston went off and I was left with the children in a Camp, which was strange and unfamiliar. When he left, Winston was very loving and promised to send for us as soon as he could sort out accommodation. I was very lonely.

For the first time I felt no excitement about my new surroundings and no illusions about a new beginning. Although I was used to being on my own with the children, this time it felt different. Padgate was a large camp and I did not know anyone there or where things/places were. However I soon found out where the local shops were. The nearest shop was the NAAFI shop, which was about a mile away. Whenever I needed anything from the shop I would have to walk down with the three children. If I needed to go into town it would involve a train journey. I would need to wheel the three children to the railway station and I would travel in the luggage compartment with Adele still in the pram. It was probably not very nice for Adele but it was the easiest way I could manage.

I gradually learned to manage the children although they could be a handful. Nowadays when I see young mothers struggling with children on buses my heart goes out to them. No one really understands how hard it really is. Besides struggling with the children I often found people looking at me in a very unfriendly way. I was sometimes tempted to ask them whether I had done something to upset them. But I knew what the issue was. A white woman with three black children, and all the prejudices and assumptions that went with it!

The weeks went by slowly. I had not heard from Winston and was worried about him. The C.O. came to see me to check if I was all right and I reassured him that I was managing. I was only just managing but my pride would not allow me to say so. I could not understand why I felt tired and run down all the time. I put it down to not eating properly as I did not seem to ever have any kind of an appetite. Anyway he went away thinking I was doing fine. A couple of weeks went by before I heard from Winston. In fact I received several letters all at once so the reason for not hearing from him was the post.

He wrote that he was in a place called Abanya in the Middle East. Much as he wanted us to be with him, there were not many

R.A.F. quarters available for families and he was trying to look for private accommodation. I read those letters over and over again feeling a real sense of closeness with him. It seemed obvious that he was missing us and I was really missing him. In our good times he was always someone I could talk to. I had no adult friends at Camp and much as I loved the children, I longed to have an adult that I could talk to. As time went by I started getting thinner and thinner. This was because I was having difficulty eating.

One day I started getting sharp pains in my chest. I was also finding it hard to manage the stairs in the house but I just ignored these signs putting it down to not eating properly. A couple of days later, whilst I was doing some washing I collapsed on the floor. I don't know what happened but I guessed I must have fainted. When I came to I struggled next door and asked the woman there if she could ask her husband to contact the doctor to visit me at home. Her husband kindly helped me out but came back with the message that the doctor would see me but I had to go to the surgery. I gathered that the doctor had been very unhelpful and so I had no alternative but to make my way to the surgery. I knew that there was something wrong with me and did not want the risk of passing out in front of the children.

I had to take the children with me, as I could not leave them on their own. I somehow got them ready and made the journey to the surgery. Desperation can make you do what might seem the impossible! When I finally saw the doctor, he said that I had Pneumonia and needed to go home and go straight to bed. I tried not to laugh. Did the man not see that I had three small children? I tried to explain that my husband was away and that I was on my own with the children – one of them being just a few months old. I needed to make up the coal fires and feed them – going to bed was impossible. The man was so unsympathetic and told me that if I was not going to listen to him then he could not treat me. There was not much point pursuing the matter so I thanked him and struggled home.

The next few days were hell as I kept fainting at the most unexpected times and I was not able to eat. This could not go on, I was frightened that I might faint whilst carrying Adele and could injure her. I had to ask my neighbours to contact the doctor again, and ask him to come and see me, as I was getting worse. This time I was lucky to get the senior doctor who was much more helpful. When he saw the state that I was in, he sent me straight to bed and got some R.A.F. boys to see to the children. The next day the doctor sent a specialist to see me who insisted that I would have to go into hospital for tests. I was terrified – what was going to happen to my children? But I guess they could not listen to my pleas, as they had a job to do.

The specialist arranged for an ambulance to come and take me to hospital and the children to be taken to a Children's Home. When the ambulance came for me I could see that the children were frightened and distressed. Both Paul and Cris were clinging to me and they had to be prised from me. All I could hear was their crying and screaming and there was nothing that I could do to help them. I was far too ill and there were no other alternatives so the children had to go to a Home. Their cries wrenched a part of me and I felt as I had failed them as a mother.

By the time I got to hospital I was in such a bad state over being separated from the children that the doctor decided to sedate me. It seemed to do the trick, because I seemed to relax and was able to sleep. The next day the lung specialist came to see me and over the next few days I had a whole series of tests done. They also told me that they had sent for my husband and he would be coming home in a few days. As soon as Winston arrived at Camp he came directly to the hospital. This was about two days later. I felt so relieved seeing him and it was quite obvious that he was really worried about me. It was so good to have someone there for me! On completion of the tests I was told to go home but to take things easy.

Although they had advised me to leave the children in the Home for a while until I was much stronger, I was anxious to get my family together again. We had never been apart and I was worried about them so Winston and I went to the Home and brought the children back home with us. It was heart warming to see their little faces light up when they saw us. They looked well enough and had obviously been well looked after but as we hugged and cuddled each other, it felt good to be a family again.

Before I could settle into a daily routine, the following week the doctor contacted me to tell me that I needed to go into hospital for further tests. These would be special lung tests. He was admitting me into West Kirby Hospital, which was an R.A.F. hospital for men. What was I going to do in a men's hospital? However he reassured me and said that they would be putting me into a side ward so that I would have my privacy. Since Winston was around I was able to discuss things with him and we agreed that I needed my health to be sorted out. Winston was very supportive which surprised me. I wondered whether being apart had done the trick! You know the saying, "Absence makes the heart grow fonder..." Anyway I was really grateful for his support as it made going into hospital easier. We were able to get all three children into a day nursery and Winston committed himself to take them in the morning and to pick them up at teatime. So I went into hospital convinced that I would be back home as soon as I was feeling strong, well and positive. After the tests the doctor came to see me. I was sure that he had come to tell me that I could go home but when he started talking I could not believe what he was saying. He was saying that he needed to do some more tests on my right lung but the tests on my left lung had confirmed that I needed an urgent lung operation. It seemed that my left lung was so badly infected that they were going to need to remove most of the lung. I was terrified! I had heard lots of horror stories about such lung operations and I knew that the survival rate was not good. Why was this happening to me? Hadn't I suffered enough already? And what about my children? What would happen to them if anything happened to me? These questions raced through my brain and I started to shake with very real fear. The tests done on my right lung were a little bit more favourable. I would need surgery in time but it was not as urgent as the left lung. That left me slightly relieved but I knew that I had a rough time ahead of me.

The doctor decided to send me home to await a bed at Broad Green Hospital. Once home and waiting to be called into hospital I felt that I was living a nightmare. Every time I looked at my three children sheer fear paralyzed me. How could I leave these innocent children to fend for themselves? Winston was being really loving and helpful but I knew this would not last. He was unpredictable and I could not depend on him to look after the interests of the children.

It was no good writing to Joe after I had refused to leave Winston I also knew that my children would have a rough time on account of colour. If I could help it, I wanted to protect them from the nastiness of the world. There were no answers and I had to just trust in God and hope that he would help me again. Within a few days I was admitted into Broad Green Hospital, onto a Heart and Lung Ward. Since I had lost a lot of weight they wanted to build me up before having the operation. However instead of gaining weight I was losing it. This was not very surprising as they used to place me in a position where my legs were raised and my head was down. This was to help my lungs to drain themselves but it made me feel sick. Besides feeling nauseous all the time, I was also very weepy. I would burst into tears for no reason at all.

When it felt that things could not get any worse, I found out that I was pregnant. What did I feel? Numbness! I could not feel any joy – all that I could think of were Paul, Cris and Adele and what the future might hold for them.

The surgeons had told me that they could not postpone the operation. They needed to operate immediately and I would stand a high risk of losing the baby. Even then I could not think about the baby. I know it sounds selfish, but all I could think of was that I was going to die!

From my bed I could watch people being taken down to theatre. I used to time them. The trolley would come to collect the person and would return in exactly 45 minutes. The trolley would sometimes be empty and I knew that person had not made it. The day before I was scheduled for theatre a woman in the ward that I was in, had gone down to theatre and I never saw her again. So I was convinced that I was going to die!

On the day of the operation I was scheduled to be the first one to be operated on. They took me down early in the morning so that I did not have much chance to panic. If it had been later in the day, I know that I would have lost my nerve. I don't remember any more that day. The next day I remember coming around and being in so much pain. I was no stranger to pain but this was different in its intensity. I was told that I had been in surgery for four hours. My body seemed full of tubes. Every time I tried to move and/or lift my arms, I felt like I was torn apart. A cut ran right across the left side of my back round to the front of my ribs. Some of my ribs had been removed. My whole body felt as if it had been ripped apart. However, one of the nice things which did happen, was that I received a letter from Winston. When I came around one of the nurses said that my husband had left a letter for me to read when I came out of theatre.

He believed that I would survive the operation! I was feeling weak and ill and it hurt me to raise my arms so that I could read this letter. So I asked the nurse whether she would read the letter to me. I cannot remember all that Winston said in the letter but it was a very touching letter. Perhaps it was the way the nurse read it or perhaps I was feeling so vulnerable that the words in the letter bounced out to wrap me in soft cotton wool and made me fell very precious. Winston begged me not to give up and to fight as getting well was important – both for the sake of the children and himself.

My husband actually said he needed me! If only he could be so caring all of the time. But I guess it was moments like this, which made me always live in perpetual hope and persevere with a relationship which seemed to be destroying me. As the days went by I did not seem to get any better – I was still in intense pain and had a dreadful cough. The surgeon told me that I was still accumulating fluid and if I did not cough it up I would need further surgery. The thought of further surgery terrified me but none of the doctors or nurses were sympathetic. I felt so ill and would be awake all night fighting for my breath. This meant that I would fall into an exhausted sleep in the morning. You would expect that the nurses would understand that I needed the sleep but their daily duties had to be completed, come what may. They would insist on straightening the bedclothes to the extent that they would pull the sheets and the sheets would cut into my wounds. If I cried out they would tell me to stop making such a fuss.

Once my sleep was disturbed it was difficult to get back to sleep, so I would once again be awake wishing for the pain to go away. I hated that hospital and to this day I have nightmares of my time there. All I wanted was to be out and back home with my family. I was now four months pregnant and had been lucky not to lose the baby. However I was still struggling to keep food and drinks down. This meant that I was still not putting on any weight for myself.

One day whilst on his rounds the doctor stopped at my bed. He did not ask me how I was but very matter of fact – like he was talking about the weather – told me that I was going to die. The fluid in my chest was blocking it and my breathing tubes. This meant that I would develop severe respiratory problems, which would end in death. I looked at him as he spoke and wanted to spit at him. Instead I internalized my anger and thought, "Blast you! You unfeeling bastard! I will not die! You might want me out of your hair but I intend to do this by walking out of this disgusting hospital. I have three children waiting at home and they need me. I am not going to die!"

My anger pushed me to stop feeling sorry for myself and spurred me on to get out of that place. The next day I forced myself to start eating a little. The nurses put up a kind of tent in the ward and I was placed in it. They had Fryers Balsam kettles boiling which eased my breathing considerably. Why had they not done these things weeks ago?

Gradually I got stronger and I was determined to convince them that I was well enough to go home. A couple of weeks later I was allowed home! I was still in a lot of pain but at least I was back home. The doctor had to call in every day to check on me. Looking back, this must have been a difficult time for Winston. He had been given leave to look after me. When he had to go back to work, the doctor arranged for a home help to come in and do a bit of housework, but Winston still needed to do the bulk of the caring. Every day he still took Paul, Cris and Adele to the day nursery. I was not the easiest person to look after. I could not lift my arms up and needed help to sit up. I was in a mess and often spent days feeling really depressed wondering whether I would ever be well again and free from pain.

I was no help with the children, as I could not do very much. Winston had to manage both the children and me. I was glad to find out that he would not be going back overseas and that he was posted back to Padgate. This made things so much easier and calmed my fears of being suddenly left alone. Now that I look back, this was about the only time that Winston did anything for us or showed us love and affection in a consistent and caring way.

Cyprus ...

September 1956. Winston was posted overseas. At the time of his leaving, all that we knew was that he was going somewhere in the Middle East. He promised to write as soon as he arrived at his destination. I was going to miss him, as the past year in Jurby had been good. I was convinced that he had now changed for the better.

I was relieved that he was going to the Middle East as at the time a lot of the services were being deployed to Cyprus. Things were tense in Cyprus because of the EOKA struggle and we had heard that men were dying every day as a result of the bullets. The news at the time focused heavily on the trouble in Cyprus and I prayed, like many other women, that my man would not be sent there.

I did not hear from Winston for a while and then all of a sudden a batch of letters came at the same time. Winston was in Cyprus and my worst fears had become a reality. He obviously could not write about what was going on.

The daily news on the radio of "...number of servicemen were shot in Cyprus..." rang in my ears. After receiving his letters I was on tenterhooks, supposedly waiting for a telegram with the bad news. Did I wish him dead? It honestly had not crossed my mind.

Perhaps if a bullet had found its mark , my story would have taken a very different path.

However, you know the saying – "the devil looks after his own" – I knew that I would not be getting any telegram. You see I knew Winston only too well. He is both selfish and very canny. He would not place himself at any kind of risk; he would take care of himself, first and foremost. Winston had said in one of his letters that the R.A.F. authorities would make arrangements for us to join him. However, he did not know when this would happen; I would just have to wait. It never once crossed my mind to say I didn't want to go; it was expected that families would want to be together and that wives would follow their husbands. And, of course, I did what was expected of me. I had to bide my time patiently as it was a bad time to travel. The Suez crisis was on, and they were using Cyprus as a refuelling stop for planes.

The British government had stopped all families from going out. It must have been around about the middle of December – I remember Christmas not being far off – that the children and I finally left the Isle of Man for Cyprus.

I was aware that it was going to be a long and tiring journey, but even I was not prepared as to the extent of tiredness. It turned out to be a nightmare! Before leaving, things were rushed and hectic. We all had to take the necessary vaccinations and the children suffered the after effects. They were all poorly with a temperature but Adele had the worst reaction. What with the temperature and the vaccinations itching, she had scratched the scab off the vaccination and developed sores all over her body. I had to call the doctor out. To make matters worse, she developed bronchitis. The doctor was very good and came in every day to dress her sores. However, she needed to be kept warm, so I had to make a bed for her downstairs by the coal fire. I had to sleep with her as she needed her medicine every few hours. I was also not feeling too good, but knew that I had no time or energy to start fussing over myself. The other children also demanded attention, I still needed to feed and look after them, as well as do all the packing and the hundred and one things which needed doing before we left the country. We finally left Douglas, Isle of Man by ship and headed for Liverpool.

By this time I was absolutely shattered and hoped to catch some rest whilst travelling. As things would have it, this did not happen. The crossing was very rough and all four children were as sick as dogs. Was I glad when we arrived at Liverpool, 4 hours late! No time to have a rest, we were rushed over to the train station to get the London train.

On arriving in London we were taken to the Union Jack club where we had sleeping accommodation for the night. The plan was that we would be flying out of the country the next day. Although we were a group of families travelling together I had no energy to socialize. I took a taxi to the club relishing the thought of a wash and something to eat. We had an early start the next day so it was going to be an early night for all of us. Arriving at the club I was relieved to find our rooms decent. I was exhausted; four children, ranging from five years to a baby can prove a handful. Much as I longed to hit the bed, I got us all washed and cleaned, went down to the dining room for something to eat, came back upstairs and we all hit the bed!

Six a.m. – I could have turned over and gone back to sleep, but I had to get up and wake the children up. We were expected at R.A.F. Hendon where we were to meet with the other families going to Cyprus.

Once the children were washed and fed I called a taxi and we made our way to Hendon. At Hendon I met the other wives and their children all due to fly to Cyprus. I was a little surprised to note that I was the only one with four children; the other women had one to two children. We were told that we would be flying from Southend airport and were bussed to the airport. You have to keep in mind that there were no motorways at the time so the journey was slow and tedious with me trying to keep four children contented and occupied throughout the journey.

I was glad when we arrived in Southend, particularly because some of the women had started to give me funny looks. All of my insecurities of not being a good mother came to the fore and I had to consciously try to ignore their looks.

The airport at Southend was fogbound and the flight was delayed. We had to hang on until they decided that it was safe to fly. It was 10 p.m. before a decision was made – by this time both the children and I were exhausted. It was decided that take off would now be tomorrow and the R.A.F. officer in charge of us decided to take us all back to Hendon. The fog was so thick that it took the bus a few hours to complete the journey. It was approximately 2 a.m before we got into Hendon. Too tired to think or even eat, I washed the children's face and hands and my own and went straight to bed. No energy to have a bath for we had to be up early the next morning.

A six a.m. start again; back on the bus and back into Southend. Surprise, surprise, the airport was still fogbound. As the weather was too bad for takeoff, we once again ended up sitting at the airport all day. I was really tired and children have a sense of knowing when you have no energy to run after them. Robert the youngest would not leave me and was extremely clingy. The other children were all running around and I could sense the disapproving looks from some of the mothers but what with Robert in my arms there was little I could do. Anyway, what did they expect? You cannot coop three active children up all day! To add to discomfort I had run out of clean nappies and clothes. We had been allowed only one bag as hand luggage and the rest of our cases were loaded on the plane. Things got so bad that the WRVS were called to come and help us out. I was really grateful for their help as they brought some nappies and a change of clothes for the children. I was feeling tired, grimy and dirty.

When we were told that we would need to return to Hendon yet again, I was at screaming point. My body felt as if it was being put through a wringer and the children were trying my patience. I knew it was not their fault but I guess when we are under pressure the rational flies out of the window. So, once again we were bussed back to Hendon; expected to be up early the next day and return to Southend.

The situation had not changed and we were left hanging around again. By this point any patience I had left snapped and I literally felt that I was climbing the walls. When they said they were taking us back to Hendon again I dug my heels in, and refused to go. Initially, they would not listen to me and out of sheer tiredness and frustration I burst into tears, saying that they would have to forcibly move me – I would not go freely. By this time I guess they realised that I was genuinely tired and upset and that they were not going to be able to persuade me to go back to Hendon.

After some time they told me that they were going to put me up in the hotel next to the airport. Why they did not do this in the first place for all the families I will never know! I found out that we were in the same hotel as the pilots and stewards and that they had decided to put all the families up in the same place. The children had eaten at the airport and were very tired so I bathed them and put them to bed. They must have been really tired because they did not fuss and dropped off almost immediately. I had a bath and tidied myself up and went down to the bar where I joined the other women and had what I thought was a well-earned drink.

The next day we sat around at the hotel lounge for most of the day and just when it was time to wash the children and put them to bed, an announcement was made over the tannoy system that we needed to be ready as we were due to take off in half an hour. Talk of sheer panic – I only had time to give the children a quick 'wipe', grabbed our things and had to dash over to the airport and board the plane.

This was the first time that I had ever flown and I was terrified. The children were too young to understand what was going on. My attention was on the children and I settled them down. Cris was very quiet and I guess he was nervous so I gave him a book to look at, and to distract him. Robert was too young to know what was going on but was incredibly good throughout the flight. After downing a few drinks I was calmer and settled down to enjoy the flight. Although some of the women were not very helpful, the majority were really good and supportive. During our long waits at the airport they had helped me out by keeping the older children occupied. I made some good friends on that trip and felt a little sad that we would lose contact before long.

When we landed in Malta I had to wake the children up, as we had to get off the plane, whilst it refuelled and was cleaned up for the rest of the journey. My first impressions of Malta were not very good. We were taken to this restaurant, which would not have won any prizes in the cleanliness department! It did not help that I could smell the toilets from where we were sitting and I decided that the children were not going to eat there. Fortunately, they were too tired to argue and after getting them a drink, we sat around waiting to board the plane. At about 7a.m. we boarded the plane and were on our way to Cyprus.

It must have been a couple of months later. The day began like most other days; getting the children off to school, making sure that the child minder had everything she needed and then getting myself off to work. When I returned home from work late that afternoon Winston was already home. This was extremely unusual and for some unknown reason made me feel nervous. I couldn't ignore him as he was sitting in the living room so I asked him if he was okay and was anything wrong.

He seemed to stare past me and had a really grim look on his face. I was really getting nervous now so I repeated myself,

"Winston are you all right? Has something happened?" The look on his face as he snapped at me to mind my own business and stop acting the considerate wife was so full of hate that I felt a shiver pass through me. As I looked at my arms I noticed goosebumps all over and furtively rubbed my skin to get rid of them. I had seen Winston in this strange mood before and knew that if I did or said the wrong thing he would explode – and with little doubt the explosion would come my way!

I decided to go about my daily chores so I went and changed into my 'home' clothes and started preparing the evening meal. The children were home so I gave them their dinner and although Winston ate with us, he did so silently. The children were fidgety and Robert was being extremely difficult. I knew that they had sensed the atmosphere and were perhaps as scared as I was. I didn't want to tell them off in case I triggered Winston's wrath. There was such a heavy brooding presence about him that I decided to finish eating as quickly as possible. After eating I cleared the table and washed the dishes before giving the children their evening baths. Winston was still sat at the table and seemed to be staring into space. I wanted to ask him if he was all right but did not dare do so. Hence I ignored him and went about seeing to the children.

Bath time was often my time with the children and was a noisy and pleasurable time. However on this day there was very little noise – I didn't have to say anything to the children –they had their baths and were keen to go to bed. Paul, however, was the only one who wanted to stay up with me and kept making excuses just so that he would not have to go to bed. I could hear Winston moving about in the next room and I was scared that he would come into the bedroom and take his anger out on Paul – you see Paul and

Winston did not get on and I often had to keep Paul out of his father's way.

I told Paul that I was going to have a bath and wash my hair and would then be going straight to bed. This seemed to reassure him and he finally went to bed. After having my bath I was in the bedroom drying my hair when Winston came into the room carrying my coat. He put it round my shoulders and said in a quiet voice, "We are going out." I was in my nightdress and said that I had just had my bath and was ready for bed.

"I don't want to go out. Why don't you go on and we can do something together tomorrow night?"

His voice became very menacing as he told me that I had no option but was going out with him – "and don't bother to change or shout out for help, no one will hear you!" It felt as if his last statement and my own thoughts collided with each other. I felt a real sense of danger and somehow knew that I would have to try and avoid getting into the car. I decided to try and start an argument in the house, as with the children next door the worst possible thing to happen would be a beating.

If I sound callous then fighting for my survival made me so. It was always a question of weighing up risks! "Where do you want to take me at this hour of the night? Are you completely mad?" I yelled at him.

He just looked at me as if I were a piece of dirt and said, "Stop yelling, woman! You will wake up my children – just shut up and get into the car. I will carry you if I have to – I am going to teach you a lesson you will never forget. I will teach you to insult me!"

I was genuinely baffled by what he was saying, it made no sense! "What on earth are you talking about? For Christ's sake tell me what I am supposed to have done?"

He just kept repeating, "You are never going to insult me again," over and over as he dragged me to the car. I was getting desperate and tried to appeal to him by reminding him that the children were left alone. He acted as if he did not hear me and started the car muttering, "I am going to teach you a lesson you will never forget..." As he revved the car up he turned it in the direction of Nicosia and started driving.

By this point I was completely petrified, I knew that I had to do something but somehow it felt as if my brain would not engage gear. All I could focus on was his threat of teaching me a lesson. I had to get away from this mad man but how? I thought of jumping out of the car but he was driving too fast for me to do so – if I fell he was quite likely to reverse over me and kill me! To describe myself as 'petrified' was a gross understatement. I now knew what people meant when they said they were 'shit scared'!

As we neared Nicosia there was a back up of traffic and we had to slow down. This was my chance! I reached for the door handle ready to jump out when he turned his head and caught my hand movement. Before I could even bat an eye I felt the full force of his fist across my face. As I reeled from the force of the blow he started the car up and moved forward. Although my face was sore and my eye was watering I just knew that this would be my only opportunity to get away. Every time the car had to slow down because of the traffic I tried to get out and he hit me across the face again. This must have happened about three to four times.

* * *

As usual Betty's face was drawn and her voice very quiet as she told me this part of her story. I had never met Winston but felt an enormous rage against him. As I sat there 'calmly' taking notes, my insides were in turmoil. The very quietness of Betty's voice portrayed her deep anguish and, again, I knew instinctively that she did not want words or actions of sympathy or comfort.

"Betty, did you not think of shouting for help? Surely someone from one of the cars would have come to help you?"

Betty looked at me and simply gave me a weary smile. "In the sanity of this room, in the middle of Stockport, yes, I could have shouted, but at the time it didn't even cross my mind. I always had to use my own resources to survive but I was also deeply ashamed about my experiences – the never-ending violence. I was always terrified that people would judge me and I was not about to announce to the world – or at least on the outskirts of Nicosia – that I was in a car with a man who was my husband and who was beating the daylights out of me. I know it sounds silly and contradicts my feelings of needing to get out of that car but I guess the feelings of shame took over the fear!"

Betty then continued.

* * *

We drove through Nicosia and out of it and were soon out in the country. I lost my bearings and all track of time. It felt as if we had been driving for hours – my mind was like a mouse in a trap – it just kept going round in a circle – got to get out, got to get out... Winston suddenly stopped the car and came over to the passenger side and dragged me out. It was as if I were in a dream, or should I say a nightmare!

I looked around me. The place was deserted and all that I could see was rows and rows of fields. A ball of fear had settled in the pit of my stomach and I wanted to throw up but did not dare do so. My mind and body felt like two separate parts, neither connecting. Winston was staring at me and I stood there waiting for the first blow. Instead, he started hurling abuse at me, spat at me and said that when he had finished with me a friend was going to come and "finish me off". I wanted to run but where to, and this might get him even more worked up!

As I stood before him, my face swollen from the earlier blows, he turned to the boot of his car and returned with a long chain. I had simply stopped feeling fear and was desperately praying the end would be quick. Winston approached me and grabbed my arms and tied them behind my back. He then calmly wrapped the chain around his fist, smiling, as if he were putting on a glove. I closed my eyes as I felt the first punch hit the cheekbone in my face. And as he continued to punch me there was little I could do to protect myself with my hands behind my back. I stopped counting the punches and the pain just became numbness. I could feel the blood dripping from my face but my eyes were shut – not because I shut them, but because of the swelling. He was a blur before me and I just wanted death to come quickly.

Suddenly he stopped and said in a very calm voice, "I think I have taught you that lesson. I am going to leave you here and my friend will finish you off, you bitch!"

As I lay on the road my body seemed to shake in spasms, my face felt wet with a sticky feeling, I wet my lips with the tip of my tongue and tasted blood. I prayed, desperately prayed that God would end it all. What kind of life was this, what kind of a woman was I, and perhaps all along I had fooled myself that my children needed me! I was the one who needed them! They were the only ones who made sense of my rotten life. It felt as if it was in the distance but it couldn't have been - a car started up. Winston probably keeping his promise to let his friend finish me off! All of a sudden there was quietness around me – no sound of a car – I thought I had finally made it, gone from this world. I then heard a car door slam and as my face felt the grit on the ground I knew that I was still very much alive! Winston had only turned off the car engine. I heard his footsteps and as I peered through my swollen eyes I saw the shoes on his feet.

"He has come to finish me off himself!"

"Come on Betty, it is time to go home. I have changed my mind and I am taking you home. I just could not leave you here, like this!"

I must have been hallucinating; this man had just beaten me up and left me for dead and he was now acting as if he was my saviour! I simply did not have the energy to respond....

Winston must have dragged me into the car. Everything was a blur – I faintly recall the journey through Nicosia and arriving back home.

He must have helped me into the house because when I was able to focus I found myself in a chair with Winston at my feet. He had a look of concern on his face.

"Betty, dear, look at the state of your poor face. What a mess? Look, you sit here and I'll get some water and a cloth and clean you up." When he left the room I got up and went to the mirror – or should I say, I stumbled to the mirror. My face was in a mess – I had not imagined it all! What was Winston playing at? I struggled back to the chair just as Winston entered the room with a bowl of water. He knelt at my feet and started cleaning my face gently, ever so gently, muttering, "Oh your poor face, what a mess!"

My stomach was churning and I wanted to throw up all over him. I wanted to rant and shout, "You did this to me!" But the only voice I had came out in a croak. All I could do was whisper, "You are sick; you did this to me you mad man. Leave me alone." He continued to wash my face as if he had not heard me and then carried me and put me to bed fully clothed. It must have been the early hours of the morning because I remember the light starting to drift through the windows, another new day but the same old story!

I have little memory of the next few days. Winston must have contacted work to tell them that I was ill and not coming in. He must have also taken time off work, as he seemed to be around a lot. I have no idea what the children thought, but I was sure that Winston would have spun out some plausible story. I remember him saying that he intended to look after me because I immediately thought 'to look after your selfish self'. You see bruised and as ill as I felt, I had not lost all reason. I knew that Winston wanted to keep me out of sight of friends and colleagues because if anyone guessed that this was his 'work' he would have been jailed. He was also terrified that I would go to the police – but I was feeling too ill and too sore to even contemplate reporting him.

After several days I was feeling a little stronger and wanted to go back to work. Winston was against this as he was obviously worried that I might report him. I could not stand him around me and desperately wanted to go back to work, as this would have given me some space. Desperation can work miracles! I somehow managed to convince him that I would not 'tell' on him and agreed that the story I would give was that I had been cleaning the verandah and fallen off it onto the gravel path, and hit a wooden box which was lying on the path. A ridiculous story I know but you would be surprised as to how many people seemed to believe it. Or perhaps they were too discreet to call me a liar to my face! Who knows?

The next day I was back at work. It was such a relief to be out of the house and to have some breathing space. People at work kept asking how I was and I kept repeating the same story like a broken record. It was difficult to make out whether they were genuinely concerned or just curious. I noticed Jane the girl next to me kept looking at me through the corner of her eye. She thought I had not noticed. Jane was one of the nicer women at work and usually spent time chatting to me. During our morning break she came up to me and asked me if I needed to talk. I tried to brazen it out and cracked some joke but I was getting tired about repeating a story that I knew was a lie.

"Betty," she said, "I am not going away. You did not fall down – your husband did this to you, didn't he?" Someone had at last said the unspeakable! It just felt an enormous relief; I didn't have to pretend any more. With my guard down I poured my heart out and told her everything. She did not say anything to make me feel judged and comforted me. Confiding in Jane made me feel as if I was not alone any longer. There was someone in my corner rooting for me. A week went by with things being very calm at home. I soon got back to the daily routine and it helped as Winston was being very charming – not that I was fooled – but anything for a quiet life.

I was still feeling weak and kept being sick but put it down to the assault. However, one day at work, some one said that I looked yellow. I laughingly responded that was my usual colour! The boss insisted that I go and see the doctor who told me that I had jaundice and needed complete bed rest. I could not believe it and felt very weary. If it was not Winston it was my health – between the two, they drained all the fight out of me. Convinced as I was, that it must have been the beating that had brought on the jaundice, I couldn't say a thing. I have little memory of this period of illness except that my kidneys had been badly damaged and I had a really bad backache that painkillers could not help. It must have been about three months before I was better to go back to work.

On my return to work everyone commented on my weight loss. At first I was taken in by their concern only to be disillusioned later. I found out by accident – actually I walked in when a group of the women were discussing me. Jane had blabbed to the rest of the women about my problems with Winston and the women were relishing in the gossip. I guess it made them feel as if they had some power over me, particularly since I had always kept myself to myself. This was a bitter lesson and I vowed never to trust anyone ever again. I did not want people pitying my children, or me or saying Winston's behaviour was typical of a black man. You know that is the first thing that people said, they always saw Winston's colour and used that as an explanation for his behaviour. It used to make me so mad but also made it very difficult to talk to anyone about what was going on in our relationship. This is why Jane's betrayal hurt so much. For the first time I tried to talk about the unspeakable only to have it thrown back into my face.

As if that was not bad enough, a few weeks later all the women including myself were given notice to leave. Negotiations had been going on to give the Cypriots their Independence and it had been agreed by the authorities to reinstate the Greek Cypriots as a gesture of goodwill. So I was once again out of a job with definite money worries looming in the background.

Living in Cyprus had a strange feeling about it. As I have already said, the people were warm and friendly but the daily violence surrounded us like a grim cloud. It cast a shadow on all our relationships never knowing whom to trust. In an ironical way the violence in the towns and on the streets reflected the violence in my home. A home is meant to be a refuge from the outside world, an haven of peace – mine was an overspill of the outside world! There was no refuge and what was worse I was often not able to protect the children from Winston's unpredictable moods. Paul always seemed to get the worst of the treatment, perhaps this was because he was the oldest and could understand some of what was going on.

Looking back I feel an enormous sense of guilt because I felt Cyprus was the start of the children's loss to a right to childhood.

The everyday killings combined with the violence in the home robbed them of their innocence – and I blamed myself for this. The continuing violence in our small village seemed to escalate just before Independence. I vividly remember an incident that involved one of Winston's friends.

He lived on the Camp and had just returned home from duty. His little boy must have asked for ice cream because he took him down to the local shop to buy some ice cream. As he was handing over his money he was shot in the back and died in front of the little boy. Everyone was horrified about the incident and in true community spirit decided to give their rent money for that month to his widow and children. My children must have heard about the incident but they never spoke of it and I often wonder what sense they made of their life in Cyprus.

When incidents like this happened I often wondered and sometimes wished that Winston would become a victim. That was one sure way of getting rid of him. I used to sometimes have terrible thoughts of how I could kill him and pretend that rebels killed him. No sooner had I had those thoughts I would give myself a severe telling off as I was fearful that my wicked thoughts might rebound on the children and me. Violence continued and when we heard that negotiations for Independence had begun we hoped that the violence would stop. This was not to be.

Indiscriminate killings were still happening. In fact on one occasion after getting a bad smell from the side of the house I thought it might be a dead dog. There was a small bridge at the side of the house and I found a sack suspended from the floor. I didn't look in it but alerted the police and they found a burnt up body of a man who had been suspected as an informer. A fleeting thought crossed my mind after receiving the information from the police – that could have been me. If Winston wished he could dispose of me just as easily. To this day I have never known why he didn't; perhaps the idea of taunting and torturing me gave him a greater kick! Just as I became used to the beatings and jibes from him I became anesthetized with the violence around me. I accepted death and murder with a nonchalance that sometimes scared me – it was simply like needing to go to the shop to buy your groceries on a daily basis! When it felt like the violence would go on forever, the British authorities announced that they were going to grant Cyprus its Independence. All detainees were released and has they made their way through the Camp they caused considerable damage. Although we lived outside the Camp we could hear the shouts and sounds of breaking glass as they wreaked havoc in the Camp. We were all advised to stay indoors as the Turkish Cypriots were furious about the Independence agreement – they felt the British had sold them out to Greece.

For some reason, and I cannot remember what, Winston decided to take the children and myself for an evening drive into Nicosia. It was the most stupid thing to do and the most frightening experience. We got caught in traffic and all around us were local Cypriots running riot – turning over cars, jumping over cars, screaming out chants of liberation and freedom. Both Robert and Adele began to cry hysterically; Cris kept saying he wanted to go home and Paul had a frozen look on his face. Winston kept yelling at me to shut the children up and I was in a state of sheer panic. How we got out of that situation in one piece I will never know. Again, someone up there must have been looking after us! Also for once Winston being black must have helped because they must have mistaken us for a local family. God alone knows what would have happened if they had found out that we were British.

Yes, life in Cyprus was unpredictable and often felt we were on one of those rides you get on fair grounds – a continuous ride of suspicion, violence and murder with a good helping of regular partying!

Partying in Cyprus

* * *

It was at this point that Betty and I took a break. I felt that I needed time out to get my head round all that happened in Cyprus and Betty was feeling both physically and emotionally exhausted. The Cyprus part of the story was in no way complete...and the story would go beyond. We agreed to meet up again in a fortnight to pick up the threads.

As I drove home from Betty's, I felt as if caught between two worlds – the relative sanity of life in Manchester and Betty's life in Cyprus. The way she talked about the violence both to herself, her children and the outside world scared me. It was as if she had no feelings, was an emotionless well with a bottomless drop. Yet I knew that this was not the case but only my perception. The feelings were there but so deeply engulfed by guilt and blame that their expression could only be seen through the reflection of the physical pain, which wracked her body. The relative safety of my personal world cushioned me against the deep emotional turmoil she would always carry with her. Like I had done so many times before I could not help myself but wonder what was it that kept her in that relationship. I knew that she often said that it was the children. But yet she knew that the violence from Winston was affecting the children negatively. And yet the children were her life in a very real way. All this seemed to be a mass of contradictions that logically I could make sense of, but emotionally found difficult to reconcile. This woman had such enormous courage and strength – she was a survivor – and yet she allowed herself to continue to be a victim. I guess that some psychologist somewhere would be able to explain this using some kind of theory. But I didn't want a theory; I did not want this woman to become an object. She was real, her experiences are real, she is a breathing living surviving woman. I had learnt to respect and love her and I wanted to be with her emotionally through this painful journey.

As I wrestled with my thoughts over the week I remembered something written by Audre Lorde about the need to speak out – and I also remembered Betty's words of having shared the 'unspeakable' with her colleague Jane. It then dawned on me that not everything needs to make sense – I did not have to agree with Betty's view of the world. No, what was important was to be able to put my view of the world on one side so as to create space to embrace Betty's. It was like playing a game of 'Shadows'. Certain shapes would mean different things to Betty and me. Like looking at clouds, I might see the shape of an elephant and Betty would see the shape of a whale. Neither of us was wrong – the only certain thing was that the shape was a cloud or a shadow. If I were to also see a whale then I would need to look at the world from where Betty was. If this all sounds cryptic then perhaps what was going on between Betty and me is also going on between the reader and myself. The one thing certain in Betty's story is that she was married to Winston and acknowledged his violence but also knew that if she were to leave him, there would be no where to go. The enormity of starting life with four young children in the early sixties was no easy matter. Betty simply had to hold onto the belief that one day some day things would get better. How or when she did not know – but they would! I now felt some of Betty's strength and instead of chastising myself for my thoughts I was able to make contact with Betty and resume work on her story with some zest and understanding. I was not going to try and 'walk in her moccasins' but to 'walk' alongside her in her journey into her past.

Betty and I met up two weeks later and she resumed her story.

* * *

It was the year of 1960. Cyprus had got its Independence and it would be several months before we returned home. I was without a job once again and there was not enough money to feed us properly. What was worse was that I was dependent on Winston again and this made life very difficult. To get money off him was a major exercise in begging and pleading. Winston was still running the car, which he had not paid for. I had washed my hands of the whole car business and therefore was not aware that he owed the car company a lot of money. To tell the truth I was not surprised as he always ran up debts wherever he was. My main concern was keeping a roof over our heads and feeding the children. We were behind with the rent and I was being constantly harassed by debt collectors, who were after Winston. He was never at home and hence I was left to face them. It was embarrassing to have to sometimes beg for credit just so that I could feed the children. It was a hard time and all our so-called friends who used to party at our house disappeared. I guess we could not entertain them so they looked for fresh pastures!

I was getting really desperate and knew that I needed a job. Prepared as I was to do anything, there were some things as a British woman I could not take on – like cleaning. Winston said this would shame him and since I was already embarrassed by the debt collectors I did not want to take on work which would open my family to ridicule. But the bottom line was that I needed a job. Things were getting really desperate and I was at my wit's end. What was I to do?

I often said a prayer asking for help from someone from above. And this help came in the strangest of ways. Winston had come home from one of his drinking sprees and started to tell me about one of the bars he had visited. The owner had told him that he was going to have to close the bar down and regretted this, as it was a good little earner. It seemed that he also had the bakery next door and was finding it difficult to manage both businesses. To pay someone to come and run the bar was not worth his while, as it would cut down his profit margins considerably. Winston had suggested that he rent it out, and he had admitted that he had not thought of renting. He was quite taken by the idea and asked Winston if he knew of anyone who might be interested. Winston had said he could not think of anyone immediately but would ask around.

That night I had a gem of an idea start to form in my mind. Why couldn't I take the bar over? Okay I didn't have a clue about bar work but I was a fast learner and could pick things up quickly. More importantly this might be the answer to our money problems. I didn't say anything to Winston about my thoughts as I was afraid that he might rubbish the idea. Instead I decided that I would go and talk to the owner the next day. I had nothing to lose and everything to gain! The next day after seeing the children off to school I went to meet with the bar owner. We had a long chat and he finally agreed to rent the bar out to me on two conditions. Winston had to agree to the lease and I would have to buy all the wines and spirits in stock. This would increase the pressure to find sufficient money and I tried to negotiate to pay for the stock in instalments. He would not hear of it and finally agreed to accept payment in two instalments. That evening I could hardly wait for

Winston to come home. I fervently hoped that he would not have gone out drinking straight from work. He finally came home and in my excitement told him about my meeting with the owner. He must have been caught up with my enthusiasm because he agreed to taking up the lease and also said that he had enough money to pay for the stock. It always amazed me as to how easily Winston could find money when it suited his own purpose. For weeks I had been struggling and he never once offered me money voluntarily. Anyway I had the sense not to bring this up and faked gratitude for his cooperation. I knew that I would have to do all the hard work but I didn't care – this was a chance to make something of a life for my children and myself.

Winston went with me to see the owner and we agreed to the conditions of the lease. The bar was now ours on rent! I could not wait to get started. There were some tables and chairs and a few glasses. The place needed a thorough cleaning as it had been neglected for some time. Several days of scrubbing and repainting the walls made the place look clean and welcoming. We had sufficient old stock of wines and spirits but needed a regular delivery of beers. With some advice from the owner I got in touch with a local brewery that agreed to deliver bottled beers three times a week. They also agreed to supply us with glasses and iceboxes but said that we needed to get a supply of ice ourselves. This was easy enough to do as there used to be lorries that delivered truckloads of ice. I contacted the relevant company and soon had the ice delivery sorted out. Some of the local men showed me how to break up the blocks of ice as they had been amused by my reaction when I saw the size of the blocks of ice. Every thing felt under control and the next important thing was to think up a name for the bar. We finally settled for the unoriginal name of 'The White Horse' and the brewery agreed to make a sign up for us.

The bar owner was a wonderful source of advice and I really don't know how I would have managed without his help. Winston was not much use; only concerned to boast about his latest enterprise and swanned around most of the time. I didn't have the time to get worked up about this as we needed to open the bar quickly – everyday it remained closed was money down the drain. The brewery completed the sign and hung it up for us. I was ever so proud to see the sign going up; hope for the future was now invested in 'The White Horse'!

It felt like ages but in actual fact it was only a few days before we were ready to open for the public. I can still remember that day as if it was yesterday. The White Horse was on the Airport Road and both servicemen on the Camp and outside the Camp would find it very accessible. Word had got out that we had rented the bar and that it was due to open soon. On the opening day the bar was full of servicemen and I was really busy. Whenever I had a minute to look around, the place was buzzing with noise – people I had never met came up to congratulate me for the good work I had done – and the bar kept attracting custom. It was one of the proudest days in my life – it felt as if things were starting to work out. It was hard graft but I have never been afraid of hard work. I was enjoying every minute of it and having some kind of an independent income helped. Taking on the White Horse had given me a new lease in life. Running the White Horse was very different from pub life in England. It was much more leisurely; people were not in a hurry to get served. For the first few weeks this was a lifesaver. If a drink had been ordered and I had no idea what it was there was always someone ready to advise me. People did not get impatient and were aware that I managed the bar on my own and would wait to be served. On some days Winston would help me, but this would only be for a short while – he would then disappear with his friends. It did not bother me as he was often more a hindrance than help, offering free drinks to friends – drinks that we could not afford to give away.

With the help of Paul and Cris I soon established a daily routine. I purchased an old second hand bike as this helped my mobility. Fortunately the bar was only down the road from our house and this made managing the home and the White Horse easier. Every morning I would get the children ready and see them off to school. I would then clean up the house and sort out food for the evening meal. It was usually about 10a.m. that I made my way down to the bar. The first thing I would do is to start tidying up and cleaning out the bar. There were always glasses left from the night before so I would have to wash them and set the bar up. Three times a week I would take delivery of the beer from the brewery ensuring that all the empties had been stacked ready to be taken away. This would bring me to about lunchtime when the bar opened up. The children would also return from school at about this time. I had arranged for the school bus to drop them off at the bar. Having a dining room attached to the bar area was very helpful. I would feed the children and they would play in the dining room while I worked in the bar. Closing time was 3 p.m. And I would spend half an hour tidying up before taking the children home. From 3 p.m. to about 6 p.m. was my time with the children. I would always make sure that they had a cooked meal and Winston would be home for about 6 p.m. I would leave the children with him and he would put them to bed. Paul was left in charge if Winston had to go out. Although I was not very happy about this there was little I could do as I needed to be back at the bar for about 6.30 p.m. Once back at the bar I would wash up from the afternoon, set the bar up and open for about 7 p.m. You know it was hard work balancing all the demands on me and keeping up with the physical tasks but I simply cannot remember ever feeling tired. Perhaps it was being my own boss, or even creating some kind of future for my children and myself but I thrived on the hard work and resulting success of the White Horse.

The reputation of the White Horse spread and we were soon getting a lot of English families coming in for an evening drink. The evenings were really busy and I sometimes felt that I could do with some additional help. But this would only eat into the profits, so I struggled on. The bar was soon very popular and with a regular clientele we were even able to start up a darts team. We started making a tidy profit but I was still very cautious as a proportion of the profits had to be invested back into the bar, mainly by building up the spirits and wine stock.

From time to time I had to leave Winston to manage the bar. This was often when I wanted to go back to the house to check that the children were all right. At first I did not notice anything undue but as I became more sophisticated in keeping account of the stock I noticed that whenever Winston was left in charge there was always a bottle of spirits missing. Sometimes he would leave an IOU in the till which was not very helpful as he never paid the money back, but at least I knew that he had taken the drink. It used to really annoy and frustrate me when drink just went missing and he would deny having taken it. Here I was, working my socks off to keep us out of debt and he was taking no responsibility at all. It sometimes felt as if he were determined to pull us down despite my struggle to keep us afloat. However I decided to let these moments of deceit go by, I was just so grateful to have enough to feed the children that I decided to settle for a quiet life.

This period in my life was relatively content. The violence at home had abated – this could have been because we hardly saw each other or that Winston did not want the embarrassment of me serving customers sporting bruises. Whatever the reasons I was glad for the relative peace and prayed that this 'calm' would continue for sometime. It was good to see that the children were also looking much more relaxed and our lives had some semblance of normality!

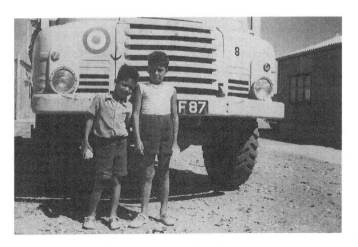

Crispin and Paul

Looking back this was perhaps one of the few times that I felt I was doing something positive with my life. However, this was not to last. Whenever things started looking positive some thing always happened to ruin it. The 'something' in this case came in the form of two Customs' men. It was soon after I had purchased additional stock for the bar. We were now well stocked with wines and spirits but our profit margin had been wiped away. I was not unduly worried as I knew that in time we would be more than making up for the expenditure – ploughing our profits into new stock was a form of an investment.

It was around lunchtime not long before I needed to open up. There was a loud thumping on the door and I went to open it, wondering who on earth was thumping at the door so loudly. There were two well-dressed men and assuming that they were customers I told them that they could come in and wait and I would serve them in a bit. They told me that they did not want serving but were Customs men checking out the licenses of all the bars in the area. When they asked to see my license I took it from behind the bar and showed it to them. My attention was on sorting out the glasses and beers, as I knew that people would soon start pouring in.

"Ma'am," one of them said, "This name on the license is Greek and I assume not yours?" What on earth was he going on about – of course the name on the license was not mine. I told him this, explaining that I was only renting the bar and that the owner had the bakery next door. They then told me that they were not interested in the owner; that as I was running the bar I needed to have my name on the license. That stopped me in my tracks, as it had not even occurred to me that I needed to change the license into my name. I was only renting the bar and the owner had not told me that this would have to happen before I could open the bar. I tried to explain this to them but they would not listen. I was starting to get frustrated and nearly in tears as I pleaded with them and told them I would send the license application off immediately. They just did not want to know. One of the men then walked behind the bar and started helping himself to bottles of brandy, whiskey and gin. He then asked the other man whether he wanted some of the left over bottles of spirit. I was really angry now, and asked them what they thought they were doing. They told me to shut up and that I was lucky that they were not clearing my entire stock or locking me up. They asked me to hand over the keys, pick up all my belongings and leave the premises. Locking the door behind them they gave me back the keys and told me that I was not to open the bar until the license had been amended. And they walked away with half my stock!

I must have cycled home but it was in a daze. All I remember is sitting in my front room feeling as if the bottom had been knocked out of my world. Sitting there I was suddenly aware of the children's voices calling out to me. The school bus had brought them home after finding the bar closed. I had completely forgotten about them in my daze. They were hungry and tired and after feeding them I let them play in the back garden. Their screams and shrieks seemed a distance away as I tried to marshal my thoughts. What on earth was I going to do? I had no excess money to buy more stock and applying for a new license would take time. In a matter of thirty minutes two strangers had walked into my life and had taken my livelihood away – or should I say my lifeline – away. Because all the profits had been reinvested into stock I was back to where I had started; not a penny better off and with all my hard work down the drain. I did not want the children to see that I was upset but I simply could not help myself. As painful reality dawned my body was racked with sobs but no tears fell from my eyes.

I knew that was the end of 'The White Horse' and the beginning of increased hardship! With the White Horse closing my life took on a different pace. However before I could adjust to the change I received another bombshell. You know I had told you about Winston's drinking sprees and how his colleagues tried to cover for him? Well, I guess they got fed up of doing so as Winston would not take any responsibility for his behaviour. One evening I received a visit from the R.A.F. Police. They were looking for Winston as he was supposed to be on duty. I did not know where he was and told them so. I might have lied to protect him but I was stunned by the visit and could not collect my wits fast enough to fabricate a story.

Anyway, they finally found him in one of the bars in Nicosia drunk out of his mind. This was a serious offence – a desertion of his post. He was arrested and held in the guardroom until trial.

How did I feel? What words can I use to express my sense of utter frustration and desolation! It was not that I felt bad about Winston being detained but the impact it had on the children. Paul particularly had a hard time at school putting up with the jibes of the other children. He also took on the role of protector over Cris, Adele and Robert – it hurt me to see my children having to deal with the shame of their father's behaviour. What was worse there was no money coming in as Winston was holding on to the marriage allowance convinced that he would be home soon.

This was not to be. His offence was viewed as serious and he was given a prison sentence and reduced in rank. The reduction in rank would have meant a further cut in his wages but the result was worse. As he was given a prison sentence his marriage allowance was stopped – this meant that literally there was no money coming into the house. I had four children to support but no income whatsoever. I wanted to remain in Cyprus until Winston had completed his sentence. With no money coming in this was proving difficult.

On the advice of the C.O. I finally decided to return to England. At least I would have access to some of the welfare benefits and would hopefully find a job. The R.A.F. put the children and me on a special plane and flew us into R.A.F. Lynemol, which was in the Blackpool area. I left Cyprus with some regrets and with only a pound note in my pocket.

Returning to England with fear at the pit of my stomach – not knowing what awaited me; not knowing how I was to support and feed four growing children – only knowing that there was no place for me and the children in Cyprus. That pound note burned a hole in my pocket – this was to be our lifeline!

Return to England

"...Life was going to be one hard slog... people
Looked at me with suspicion... the children had no-one except me
and that was scary..."

It was a cold dark afternoon when Betty and I next met. Betty
had drawn the curtains of the front room and the lights from a
lamp cast a warm glow in the room. She insisted on making me
a cup of tea and whilst in the kitchen we talked about mundane
things. I could see from Betty's face that she was in considerable
pain – she was pale and her skin looked pulled over her facial
bones.

When asked how she was, as usual she played her pain down
and cracked a joke about getting 'high' on her 'pills'. I wanted to
know if she was well enough to continue with her story, and she
insisted that she was all right. Although I had a feeling that this was
not entirely true I respected her wish to continue. You see this play
for time was part of our relationship. Betty was a proud woman
who did not like to distress others by showing her pain.

* * *

As the plane touched down on the tarmac, I looked out of the window. It was dark out there with dots of light forming a dancing pattern on the dark backdrop. Beacons of Hope? The darkness reflected what I was feeling deep down inside – and part of me hoped desperately for the flickering beacons of hope. The children were asleep except for Paul. I don't know whether he read the fear in my eyes but as soon as the plane stopped and he could free himself from his seatbelt he leaned over and hugged me and whispered, "Mum, it is going to be alright." I don't know whether he remembers this, but I have never forgotten *he* was my beacon of hope.

The plane landed at R.A.F. Lynemol where I knew that we had to stay the night before commencing our journey to Blackpool. Why Blackpool? You know I am not really sure – I think it had something to do with the R.A.F. and where they could offer us accommodation. Anyway we were taken to the overnight quarters and told to be ready to leave by early morning. The children were so tired and resistant to having a bath that I put them straight to bed. I sorted out things for the morning, had a wash and hit the bed.

I was awakened by Robert, who was complaining that he was hungry. Strange – how I remember that. Anyway we all got up, had something to eat and waited for the transport. The bus picked us up and took us to another R.A.F. station. From there someone took us to the station and put us on the train to Blackpool. It just felt as we were constantly moving and it did not help that the children were starting to get ratty. I guess they were tired and bored, and I had no toys or games to keep them occupied. The train journey was tedious and I just wanted to get to our destination and settle in.

Anyway it gave me time to plan my strategy and decide what I needed to as a priority. First thing was to get the children into schools, or should I go and see the Social Welfare? I decided to do both at the same time, although getting the children into school was important as it would free me up to look for work. I knew that I had to be prepared to take up any kind of work, but I was not proud and hard work never frightened me. In fact it provided some relief – and the more mindless a task the better.

I cannot remember how long the journey took but we arrived in Blackpool by late afternoon. Blackpool station was simply bustling. It felt strange getting off that train and mingling amongst the milling crowd of holidaymakers. They had all come here to have a good time. We had to be there for our survival! Blackpool was a holiday resort; the place for working class families to have a holiday break. It was just the start of the season – here I was wearing a hat and suit, my children in semi formal clothes which were creased by the long journey, and around us were people in summer clothes and flip flops. It made me smile; it was hardly warm enough but it was all part of the 'holiday game'. I looked at the children and their eyes were jumping around as if they were in some strange land. Adele became fixated by a brightly coloured towel and bucket and spade and wanted to make friends with the child carrying these 'goodies'. I saw the curious look flit over the child's face, she touched Adele's face and the screamed out for her mother. My stomach dropped as I saw the confusion in Adele's face but hurriedly told Paul and Cris to hold onto our luggage, clutched Adele and Robert's little hands and made a determined move to the exit.

We had to wait near the exit, as someone was to pick us up and drop us to our lodgings. I had no idea what this was to be; only aware that the R.A.F. was expecting us to refund all the rent money as soon as Winston was released. I tried not to be aware of people's glances and looks – I was determined not to feel ashamed or strange.

A man in uniform came over and said "Mrs. Jones?" and I smiled in relief. At last we were on our way, for better or worse. The hotel, or more correctly, boarding house was on the south shore of Blackpool. It was near the sea front and fairly central to the hustle and bustle of thriving holiday resort. As we drove to the boarding house I inhaled the smells around me, so peculiar to Blackpool. Smells which mingled – sea and salt, sea gulls and fried food. In a strange way it was comforting and seemed to envelop all of us, making us feel as we were indeed back 'home'.

Cris, Adele and Robert were clearly excited, as they all had loved the sea in Cyprus. Even Paul had relaxed visibly and there was almost a holiday feeling in the car. All through the journey they kept asking, "Mum, can we swim...Mum, can we...Mum, please let us." I loved their ability to bounce back, their resilience and determination to have a good time, whatever. We arrived at the boarding house and the landlady met us and took us to our room. Yes, it was one room, but I had no intention of complaining as it was going to cost us at some stage.

The man from the R.A.F. reminded me of the conditions, namely that this was only in the form of a loan –the rent would have to be paid back. With the rent came two meals, breakfast and tea. I felt a sense of relief, as I was worrying about money for food and I didn't like to ask. This meant that we could feed ourselves without draining any money I earned. After he wished us good-bye I had a proper chance to look around.

I was aware that the R.A.F. used the boarding house to lodge families who were waiting for overseas postings. It was temporary accommodation and this meant that all the families in there were in transit. This meant that I was not going to make any friends, just lots of acquaintances – but then that was the story of my sorry life! As always I tried to look on the bright side of things and thought it would save money as socialising can get expensive. The room itself was adequate and clean. It would be cramped but we would manage. The children were keen to unpack and go out exploring and I had to work hard at calming them down. You know, as I started unpacking our bags, taking out only what was necessary, I looked over. All four children were looking out of the window with Adele giving a running commentary and Robert trying to keep up.

* * *

"Four beautiful children, so innocent, somehow trapped with me in this loveless marriage – but they never had the choice." Betty's face was drawn in pain and a tear struggled in a bedraggled fashion down a face which although tired, emanated with inner strength. I simply held her hand. "Now that I can look back I often wonder what my children really think of me. At the time I carried around with me a sense of guilt but never really examined it. I could not. I had to believe that all I did was with the children foremost in mind. It is only now I wonder – was it the children or myself that I was thinking of. Would it have been different if they had been white? Maybe I would have been able to set up home independently more easily but then again, maybe I am just fooling myself! Maybe I was just a weak person. I don't know. I had survived without Winston and in fact we had a better life when he was not around – yet I still believed I needed him. I think it was the long silence – not having another adult to talk to – at least when Winston was around I did not feel totally responsible. Oh, it is all too difficult; I just hope that my children as adults will understand. I never meant to hurt them – they are my life."

* * *

Anyway, that one room soon became home. I managed to get all the children into school. This freed me up for the day. The only work available was cleaning, so I became a cleaner for several of the hotels and boarding houses in the area. The Social was only giving me family allowance, but as always I was grateful. Cleaning was hard work – grotty rooms, demanding owners and landladies, and some people were never satisfied. You were often treated as dirt, but I never complained, simply because I could not afford to. If you developed a reputation for being difficult you would not get work because word would get round.

The children settled in school and we plodded on. Every night I worried about money and the growing rent debt. An unexpected expense was food. Although we had food provided the portions were meagre and my children were always hungry. So I had to supplement the food with sandwiches and soup and other bits and pieces. Also being in Blackpool in season was problematic. Everything was so expensive. Just basic things like toiletries and travel seemed to eat into the money I made each week. The harder I seemed to work the faster the money disappeared. Over the weekends we would all go down to the beach but the children wanted to do things like go to the funfair. I was not able to refuse them as I felt that they were entitled to some fun. But it made things hard.

We soon got into a routine and must have been there for about four months when I heard that Winston was on his way back to us. I could not believe it; but why was I surprised? He had managed to charm his way around the authorities, probably made up some story about us – who knows – but he was on his way back home. Winston was back with us. When I heard that he was on his way to England I felt very confused. Part of me looked forward to his homecoming – at least I would not be on my own; people might stop treating me with suspicion – and it would be nice to have someone to talk to. But on the other hand, I was scared. What could I expect? A bitter man who might want to vent all his frustration at us? I simply could not settle, fluctuating between fear and relief. The children must have sensed my uncertainty and really played up – they challenged me constantly and pushed me to my limits. It felt as if they were testing me.

Looking back now, perhaps I should have talked to them and found out how they were feeling about their father's return, but I did not. Perhaps I was afraid to listen to what they had to say, perhaps I did not know what to say to them; whatever the reason, we never discussed Winston's return. There was just a general acceptance that he would be back with us soon.

The Winston who returned seemed a little strange. He was pale and had lost weight. Looking very subdued, he greeted us with open arms. His face seemed to say that he had genuinely missed us. I can't remember if he brought any gifts for the children but I can remember the tears in his eyes when he said "I missed you." Whether this was another game or not, I did not want to test it out. I was just grateful to see a 'changed' Winston, more humble and gentle.

As the days went by he did seem different. We had no arguments or fights and he took his share of looking after the children. The two younger ones seemed to enjoy his company, but Cris and Paul were a little reserved. Many a time I caught Paul looking at his father with very real resentment. But as usual I avoided confrontation and did not talk to him about his feelings. Selfish? Yes, I now see that I was, but I really did not want to rock the boat and do anything to trigger Winston off. At first, although I felt that I was walking on eggshells, I started to relax and enjoy this 'new' Winston. I guess it was just as well that we got on. Living and sharing one bedroom was hard and if there had been conflict it would have been intolerable.

This was a happy time in my life. It felt as if we were courting again. We had some good times going to the beach, taking the children out to the fair or a walk, on some days, just the two of us, taking an evening stroll down the promenade. Yes, those were good times. I still went out to work and was the only person working but I accepted this. I brushed to one side my concern that Winston did not seem bothered that we owed the R.A.F. a lot of money. I was just contented that my husband had changed for the better – prison had seemed to do the trick.

Although financially times were very hard, emotionally I was contented and started feeling a sense of peace. It must have been several weeks before Winston heard that he would be posted in Norfolk. He was excited and keen to go and make a start. It seemed practical that he went ahead and sorted out accommodation for us – we would then join him. I actually was sorry to see him leave and dreaded the lonely nights. He promised to contact us as soon as he had found a house.

It was about a week and a half later that he wrote to say he was missing us and that he had found somewhere to live. The R.A.F. had offered him a house but it was in a state and needed work doing to it. As soon as that was sorted out we would be able to join him.

Two further weeks went by; our debt to the R.A.F. was growing steadily, and the children kept asking, "When are we going, Mum?" and my patience was running thin. I knew that if I did not do something desperate we could be in Blackpool for months. I talked to the children about what I planned to do and why I was doing it. They treated it as a game and were keen to get it underway. We bundled some of their clothes into plastic bags and made our way to the R.A.F. office. I asked to see the CO. When he called me into his office, the children followed me in. I dumped the plastic bags on his desk and told him that those were the children's clothes. I said that I was fed up of waiting for things to happen and could not afford the lodgings anymore. I could manage on my own as long as the children were safe. Therefore I was going to leave the children with him until the house in Norfolk was sorted.

At this point both Robert and Adele started to cry. Were they playacting? To this day I do not know – but it seemed to do the trick. Yes, I know that I took a risk; I had not even thought about the possibility of the CO contacting the Social Services. God alone knows what I would have done if that had happened. Anyway, he probably was so terrified about being left with four children under twelve that he promised to make sure things were sorted out quickly and also said that the R.A.F. would meet the rent costs of the lodgings from that date. What a relief!

Soon after we received notice that the house was ready and that we could move in. As I started packing our things I found out that Winston had been up to his old tricks. What is that saying that "an old dog can..". When we were returning to England Winston had convinced me to carry our record player and records back with me. He said that a player would cost a bomb. So it made some sense; we carried this player instead of the children's games and toys. I had it stored by the landlady.

When I asked for it back, she told me that Winston had asked for it some time ago. Putting two and two together I realised that he had sold it. What he did with the money I never knew, but as usual I struggled to feed and clothe us and he just abused my trust. I was furious but I guess this was another bitter lesson I did not forget. But I convinced myself that as long as he was not violent I could cope with anything. And so we made our way on a long tedious train journey to Norfolk and a 'new' life.

Winston met us at the station. He tried to warn me about the house but I was too tired to listen. When we arrived the house looked fine but the garden was overgrown. It was a cottage style house – the old fashioned married quarters. I knew that the bathroom and toilet would be downstairs with the bedrooms upstairs. The children were excited because there were open fields behind the house. They wanted to go and play so I agreed, asking Paul to keep an eye on Adele and Robert.

Was I glad that they were not with me when I walked through the front door! The house was in a mess and that is putting it politely. It had a strange smell and I felt irritated with Winston that he could not have bothered to clean it. I can not remember what we did that night but my memory of the next day was getting down to making the place habitable. I guess I had been in worse places, particularly thinking of our accommodation in Manchester. As I have said before, hard work never frightened me and I looked forward to making this into a home.

It took a few weeks to sort it out. What really surprised me was that Winston made time to help. In the past, he always saw the house as my domain and responsibility and would get irritated if I asked for help. This time he was there whenever I needed a hand, and I did not even have to ask. I had no intention of questioning this and just enjoyed being a family without fear of abuse or violence.

We scrubbed that house from top to bottom until we got rid of the musty and rotting smell. Some of the cupboards were smelly and broken. Winston pulled them out and replaced them and even painted the new cupboards. Some of the furniture had to be burned and the R.A.F. replaced bits and pieces. This house soon started looking like 'home', and it was all the more precious because it had involved both Winston and I working as a team.

When Winston was like this, life seemed to have some kind of purpose. We felt like a real family and the children seemed to love it. They had loads of space to play – what with the open fields and trees to climb – they never missed not having lots of toys. They made the most of what was around them.

The first few weeks were idyllic and I was happy. Once I had settled the children down in school I knew that I had to find work. Winston's salary was not enough, and the fact that he had been demoted and had a pay cut did not help. However I did not want to harp about the past, so I decided to look for work. Being desperate I could not afford to be choosy. For a while I worked in the NAAFI shop. I purchased a bicycle and in the morning would cycle down to the shop and open it. We sold everything there – from a toothbrush to a washing line! We also provided food to men billeted there. Hence I not only served in the shop, but served food and did the clearing. My day would start early in the morning until about 4p.m. I would then return home and make the evening meal. The children would be home from school and I would get them washed and fed before leaving for the evening shift. I would then return home after 11p.m.

The only way I could hold down this job was with Winston's help. He agreed that on the nights I worked late he would look after the children. I felt that I could trust him as I was convinced that he had indeed changed. The more fool me! I only found out much later from the children that he often went out after I left leaving them on their own but making sure he was back in time for my return home.

Besides working at the NAAFI I also did some fruit picking. Most of the wives on the base did this to earn some extra money. Although it was hard work I loved being in the open air feeling Spring and Summer around me. It was often quiet in the fields with only the gentle murmur of our voices. Occasionally someone would burst out in laughter and the sound would ripple around us.

During the school holidays the children would join me and we would often have a picnic to break up the day. Although things started being a bit up and down between Winston and me it was a relatively quiet time of my life. He did the usual lying and drinking but I was able to tolerate this as long as he did not hit me or the children. We seemed to have arrived at some kind of plateau in our relationship – a kind of silent agreement – and I was not going to do anything to cause eruptions. I just wanted to enjoy my family and home.

A Silent Agreement, Norfolk, 1961

We must have been in Norfolk for a couple of years when Winston's brother-in-law, Bami, came on a weekend visit. I can remember it as if it were yesterday. Winston came home with a letter from Bami. He was coming to Britain to organise the Sierra Leone Independence Ball. Since he was in London he wanted to come and visit us and meet us. I was really nervous as this was the first of Winston's relatives I had met – what would he make of me – would I impress him and how did he feel about his brother marrying a white woman? These questions hurtled through my mind like a high speed train; I tried to talk to Winston, but he could not take my fears seriously. He was anxious to impress Bami and made sure that I had thought about meals and how we were to keep him entertained.

Bami was a really nice man. When I met him I knew that I had worried unnecessarily. He welcomed me into the family and took a great interest in the children. I only knew this man for a weekend and yet it felt as if I had known him all my life. There seemed to be a common bond between us and I could talk with him as I had never been able to with Winston. He told the children about Sierra Leone and he spoke about the country with such passion that I longed to see it. Little did I know at the time that he was going to be an ally when I had nobody else in my corner.

The weekend went far too quickly and I was disappointed that he had to leave. You can imagine both Winston and my excitement when he invited us to the Ball. I loved music and dancing and hadn't been out for ages – now I was going to a V.I.P. dance. I could not contain myself and saw Bami departing with some regret. However we would all be meeting up in London that weekend. I knew that I had made a lifelong friend and a true friend in Bami. Before leaving he took me aside and told me to contact him if I ever needed help. To this day I wonder whether he knew what Winston was really like! I never ever asked and he never said.

It must have been 1961 or 1962. My memory is not too good and I get a little confused with time. This might well be because time had little relevance – my experiences all seemed to merge into one.

Time was only important in the context of my children growing up. As they grew older, my experiences with Winston became their experiences with him.

After Bami left, the house seemed very empty. Although things were not bad with Winston there was a certain distance between us. I had the children and my thoughts and he had his social life! With Bami's invitation to the Independence Ball I had something to look forward to. We could not really afford it, but I was tired of scrimping and scraping. I decided that I was going to the Ball with Winston even though I knew that he would have preferred to go on his own. Bami had invited me and I was going.

* * *

Betty gave me a wry smile. "I could be very stubborn, you know. Anyway I loved music and dancing and since Cyprus I had not been out socially. My life was around the children and daily chores. This was my chance to have some fun – and by heck, no one was going to stop me!

"The Independence Ball was being held at the Guild Hall in London and Bami had warned us that Royalty would be present. We did not have appropriate clothes and decided to hire them whilst in London. We travelled up to London from Norfolk. The children were really excited – I guess train journeys always thrilled them – made them feel that they were on some kind of an adventure. In London we were to stay with some of Winston's cousins. We knew that the house would be crowded but we were only going to be there for a couple of days. Bami was sorting out our clothes. Just thinking about it, I wonder whether Winston ever paid him?"

Betty shook her head – "I am drifting ...... now where was I?"

* * *

The train journey was uneventful and we finally got to the house. I was nervous as this was my first meeting with the family. I kept my fingers crossed that I would remember names and fervently hoped that the family would like me. Bami was there to welcome us – seeing him made me relax – particularly as he warmly welcomed us.

It is at times like this that children can be wonderful in breaking up tension or discomfort. After some initial hesitancy and shyness they started playing with some of the children in the house and as their voices mingled, the adults started to talk and our voices soon sounded relaxed and there was a harmonious buzz.

The house was very busy and crowded but it had a nice feel about it. Winston's cousins were warm and treated us as family. I knew that the children would be all right on their own - the older children would keep an eye on them. They looked so happy and relaxed that I felt a pang of guilt. Besides having each other they had little contact with other children; with moving around they had little chance to form any lasting relationship. They just looked so happy that I momentarily wondered what we were doing to these four beautiful children. Just as quickly as the thought flashed through my head, I put it out of my mind.

This was no time to be morose and I was determined to have fun. Amidst all the hustle and bustle and hectic activity around getting ready for the Ball, I noticed Winston in deep conversation with one of his cousins. Her name was Felicia and she was a single parent with three children. Winston seemed to be spending a lot of time with her and had a look about him which made me very aware that he was charming her. I felt a bit irritated as even in the bosom of his family he could not behave himself. Anyway, I told myself off for having a suspicious mind and also for being a little jealous every time I heard her peal of laughter echoing in the room.

The Ball was wonderful. It was just like one of those scenes you see on films; the strains of the waltz swinging around the room, men looked distinguished in evening dress, women heavily scented in beautiful ball gowns and immaculately coiffured hair. I really felt like Cinderella at the ball. And what a smashing time I had! I danced till my feet ached, got heady on champagne and flirted shamelessly. It was the party of my life and I loved every minute of it. I was no longer boring, downtrodden Betty Jones – as my feet moved to the rhythm of the Foxtrot I felt beautiful, desirable and at peace with myself.

* * *

As Betty talked her face was flushed and animated. In a strange way she was no longer the tired pain-filled woman sitting across from me. She became the picture on the mantelpiece – tall and beautiful with a body which moved to the rhythm of music –someone who loved life and who life loved!

Tall and Beautiful

It was at this point of the story that I saw a 'Betty' who I had never really seen. It was her zest for life which made her the survivor she was. Her gentleness pulsated with life and her story now took on a new perspective. She was a human, living being who took from life what was given and in all this was a fighter with a spirit which would not be defeated! Betty was no longer simply the frail looking woman –under that fragility lay a woman with enormous strength, vivacity and an incredulous audacity. She was not just wife and mother but living, breathing WOMAN.

Betty continued her story a few weeks later when we met again.

* * *

On our return to Norfolk I soon settled into my daily routine but that weekend in London will always remain with me. It also had an impact on the children as they would often talk about their 'cousins' in London. We must have been back for a couple of weeks when I had a surprise visitor. Surprise is perhaps understated! Remember me telling you about Winston's cousin Felicia – well, it was her with her three children! Little did I know that when I opened that door and welcomed her that it was going to be the beginning of another nightmare and painful episode of my life with Winston.

At first I thought that she had come for a break, particularly since she said that Winston had invited her over. For the first week nothing untoward happened although I was starting to panic again about how we would manage if she decided to stay longer. I tried to talk to Winston to find out how long she was going to stay, but he got very angry with me and told me not to be 'English'. Africans always accommodated family irrespective of their circumstances.

It was when the week stretched to two that the problems started. She slowly started to take over, deciding on meals, wanting me to give her money. She began to go out with Winston in the evenings leaving me with the children. Many a night I lay in my bed with tears running down my tired cheeks, fiercely angry, listening to their laughter and silences which did not leave much to the imagination.

On some nights they would get me out of bed and demand that I cooked for them and would continue drinking whilst I got their food ready. If the food did not suit her, she would swear at me, sometimes throwing the food at me – and all the time Winston simply laughed. Laughter is supposed to convey happiness – all that his did was convey scorn and derision; making me feel dirty and ashamed. Initially I did not fight back as I did not want the children to be upset; after all, to them their cousins had come to stay and they had playmates.

One night I simply cracked up; after listening to her abuse and being told to get out if I didn't like it, I snapped. This was my house and my family – she had no right to it – and so I yelled back telling her to leave and get out. I don't quite remember what happened then but I have a vague memory of a tussle and suddenly finding myself out of the house with Winston's laughter bouncing discordantly in my ears.

I had to sleep in the garden that night and was only allowed in when it was time to get the children up. My body was stiff and damp with the morning dew and the coldness seemed to seep deep into my bones. I was trembling, not with cold or fear, but with sheer anger. It was my efforts which put food on our tables, it was my efforts which had made us a home and nobody was going to take it away from me! I saw Winston before he left for work and told him in a quiet voice that if she was not out by the end of the day I was going to see the CO. Perhaps it was my tone of voice, perhaps it was because he was in enough trouble with the R.A.F., whatever the reason, Felicia and her children moved out that evening. And that was where the real nightmare began.

Initially when Felicia and her children moved out, Cris, Adele and Robert kept asking me where they had gone. I felt incredibly guilty about pushing them out and depriving my children of the company of their cousins, but it needed doing. Winston was being extremely hostile to me but as long as he did not hit me I felt that I could handle things. This man had put me through a lot and I should have hated him. Part of me did but a part of me still loved him. It was this small part that kept me hanging onto a farce of a marriage.

Once Felicia moved out I decided that I was not going to ask Winston about her whereabouts and I acted as if she had never been around. You must wonder at my naivety – I often wondered about it myself! Anyway it was only a couple of days later that I found out that she had hired a cottage in Stanhoe not far from the base. I wondered how she had found the money to do this but assumed that Winston in his usual devious way would be paying for it. More fool me! That was when the nightmare really started.

At first she kept sending her eldest son to our house to get coal and food. Much as I was struggling to feed my children I could not say no, because I was concerned for her children. I knew what it felt like to be alone with no support and I guess I felt that I could be generous now that she was out of my house.

Winston then started spending a lot of time away from home, often not returning at night. I knew that he was with her and it hurt. What really hurt was the fact that by now I had made friends at the Camp and people knew us as a family. Soon people were gossiping and she was often referred to as his 'other' wife. I hated the pitying looks and the fact that no one said anything to my face – it was in their eyes...the pity!

I might have been able to handle this but it got worse. I started receiving demands for rent of the cottage. When I checked it out I found out that she had put my name down on the rent agreement. Not only were there demands for rent but tradesmen started turning up at my door with demands to pay their bills. Everything was in my name! They would not listen to me, all they were concerned about was getting their money. I did not dare say anything to Winston as I was afraid that the violence would start all over again. I also knew that there was little point in trying to talk with her, and so every time there was a knock on the door I hid and would not answer it. My children must have thought me crazy. I felt like I was going out of my mind and lived with fear every time someone came to my front door. I was expecting the law to turn up at any time. Here was I struggling to feed and clothe my children – I never saw the colour of Winston's money and we had to live on my wages – and I was 'getting' further and further into debt although it was not of my making.

Things were reaching breaking point, when Winston came home one day and told me that we were to be posted to Shropshire. We would have to move in a couple of weeks so I had to get things sorted. Much as I was tired of moving and wondered why we were being posted elsewhere I was relieved. This was one way of getting rid of Felicia and the problems she created.

Before leaving a posting it was our responsibility to put our quarters in order and return it with all its contents. Felicia had helped herself to several items from our quarters and I knew that I would have to get these things back. I tentatively asked Winston if he minded talking to her and getting back the stuff but he got very angry with me and started shouting at me to do my own 'dirty' work. I was too scared to pursue the matter and decided that I would have to see Felicia myself. Initially I toyed at the idea of taking the children with me and pretending that we had come to say good-bye. It was tempting but I finally told myself not to be a coward and that it was not fair on the children. They were confused enough about the whole episode but were also very upset about moving, and a visit to Felicia might make things more difficult. So gritting my teeth I made my way to the cottage.

She was very cold when she saw me but her eyes were blazing. I will never forget those eyes. The moment I told her that we were leaving I knew that she had known all the time; Winston must have told her. I tried hard to stop my voice from trembling and said that I needed the things from our quarters back. It was as if I had suddenly unleashed some terrible force. She started yelling and swearing at me, telling me how Winston had been sleeping with her and how he hated me and wanted to be with her. She pushed me out of the front door and soon started throwing the things I had wanted out of the house.

As I picked up things like cutlery, an iron etc. I felt very tired. I knew from her reaction that Winston had dumped her and part of me felt sorry for her. But overwhelmingly, I felt tired...really really tired......Much as we had had some good times in Norfolk I was glad to leave. I no longer thought of 'fresh' starts but was just relieved to leave bitter endings behind. Any dreams I ever had were left in those married quarters in Norfolk – I vowed again that all my hopes and energy would be invested in my children and not in the ashes of a dead marriage.

We moved to the new posting in Shropshire. It was about this time that Winston told me that he wanted to go home to Sierra Leone and that he had started applying for jobs. Bami was to put in a good word for him and he was therefore hopeful. There was no discussion about it, about what I wanted, about what was good for the children – just that we were going! This was typical of Winston; his needs always came first. I did not know how seriously to take him and so put this announcement to the back of my mind. My priority was settling the children in and getting a job – the rest could follow in what ever way life decided to pan itself out.

The married quarters were all right although very cold. It was the beginning of a vile winter – pipes were always getting frozen. We had no real heating except for a coal fire in the living room.

I very quickly got a job in a transport cafe just outside the camp. It was on a main road and easy to get to. I worked from 10a.m. to 6p.m. and it was hard work. As usual I soon established some kind of routine which often gave me little time to myself. In the mornings I would get the children ready for school and after they left I would clean and tidy the house and lay a fresh fire for when Winston came home for 4.30p.m. I would then go off to the cafe returning home on my bicycle for about 6.30p.m. Winston was not prepared to help, so no sooner did I get home I would have to make the tea and sort the children out with their baths etc. After having his tea Winston would usually be out for the evening. I was past caring where he went and with whom! The routine was heavy and monotonous but I guessed it would not be for long. Winston was also going up to London a lot; he said it was for interviews. I just accepted this as most of my energy was taken up with my children.

It was not long before Winston got a job offer from a Diamond Mining Company in Sierra Leone. Somebody must have been pulling strings for him. When he told me the news and said that he had given his notice to the R.A.F. I knew that Africa had become a reality. How did I feel about going to Africa? Terrified. Much as I loved the idea of travelling and the thought that my children would be in touch with an important part of their heritage, I was terrified. I did not want to go. It was like stepping into the unknown; into territory which entirely belonged to this unpredictable man that I had married. Oh, he said that Bami would be there and that his family were looking forward to us moving there but how could I believe him? Winston could always dress up the truth – he was a master at it. I desperately tried to talk to him. This was when I found out that he had decided to return to Sierra Leone not because he wanted to but because the R.A.F. were fed up of him and were intending to kick him out. Hence the move to Shropshire! They had given him the option of leaving voluntarily or be discharged. To this day I do not know if this was the truth but it was enough to panic me. An unemployed Winston terrified me. He also made it clear that if I did not go, he would take the children with him and I would never see them again. These might have been empty threats but I had learnt what Winston was capable of and this threat sounded very real. However the thought that the children would be surrounded by extended family who loved them was enticing – you see the time in London with Bami and Winston's cousins was still indented in my mind. I agreed to go.

Once I made the decision I got on with the practical tasks of packing our belongings in tea chests ready to be transported by sea. As our belongings went into those chests it felt as if I were slowly packing bits of myself. This move to Africa was for real. There was no turning back. I had already lost all contact with my family – my children did not know their uncles and cousins from my side of the family; I would not be leaving behind any loved ones, only the familiarity of England and a host of memories. Yes, I would be at Winston's mercy but what was so different? I had always been at his mercy – isolated and alone. I might be even more alone in Africa but at least there might be a chance of allies in his family. Anyway, the children were really excited at the prospect. For them it was another adventure; but then again, I just assumed that they were excited – never thought to ask them how they really felt. I guess that in all this I had to believe that this move was in their best interests – having no real choice I simply could not afford to believe anything else.

Leaving those cold quarters in Shropshire and beginning our journey to Africa, I realised that I had no regrets; only an enormous sense of fear of the unknown. At least my children were to be embraced by a continent, a country which would welcome them, where cold stares and rude remarks would be something of the past. I hoped and fervently prayed that this would be a new beginning for them – I had no illusions about Winston or myself. But for them – I wanted Africa. Africa would give them sunshine and warmth which would ease all tensions, the sun would kiss their skins and wrap them in an all -embracing hug, so that they at last would truly feel a sense of belonging!

Journey to Africa

My struggle
I arrived in Africa feeling lost,
and little did I know the cost this
beautiful dark continent would bring.
My marriage broken, my children afraid,
I had to return from whence I came.

We boarded the ship and we came to these shores
where everyone seemed to be closing their doors.
We tried oh so hard to be friendly and nice,
but I found that I was paying the price for
marrying a man who was not very nice.

I prayed so hard for God to give, me
courage, strength and will to live.
Well the struggle was great and the years have rolled on
and my children have married one by one.
Now my work on earth is done.

Journey to Africa. . .

" ...A new beginning...no! I no longer had any illusions or dreams. They were all dead —killed by Winston's brutality. But I did have hopes for my children ... now they were to be part of a family...to have come home...I was now to be the stranger..."

* * *

We left England at midnight. The company paid for our airfares and would provide us with accommodation in Sierra Leone. I now knew that Winston's cousin worked for the Company and had probably pulled a few strings to get Winston the job. With Winston's track record I could not believe any sane person would offer him a job. As the plane flew out of London the sky was pitch black; the darkness formed a comforting cushion – reassuring and warm.

It was wonderful watching the children. Robert was drowsy but the excitement of his brothers and sister kept him up. This was all an adventure for them. Their innocence and acceptance of change touched me. I knew that I had to keep any feelings of foreboding or worry to myself. Anyway their excitement was infectious and I also wanted to keep it going for as long as possible.

I've lost track of time but it must have been about 1963. Robert the youngest would have been about 8 years old and Paul the eldest about 12/13 years. I can remember Winston being very nervous, as it was about 16 years since he had returned home. In different ways this was all a new experience to each of us. Sitting on the plane I was tempted to ask Winston whether he had ever imagined returning to Sierra Leone with a white wife and four children. But I knew better than to put into words some of his fears. We were to fly into Freetown. Winston had told me about Freetown and its history and connections with the slave trade. This was during the good times with him – when he wanted to share his past and his history.

I knew that we were to meet his parents and family in Freetown before going to the Mine. What did I feel? Nervous I guess ...but then who wouldn't be? I still held onto the memory of Bami's family and the warmth of their welcome in London. They were a part of Winston's family so although nervous I was not afraid. I really wanted to ask Winston whether he had told them that I was white, but was scared. Anyway I had assumed that Bami would have told them, and once they met my four wonderful children the coldest heart would be won over.

The flight, which at first seemed uneventful, all of a sudden became a nightmare. One minute we were flying smoothly and the next we were asked to put on our seat belts and remain seated. We had flown right into the pathway of an electric storm. It was terrifying – it felt as if the thunder would never stop and the flashes of lightning were far too close for comfort. The children were excited; I guess to them it was like being in the middle of a film-set or a giant bonfire in the sky. It didn't help me – every time they drew my attention to the flashes of lightning I could only clutch the edge of my seat, praying fervently. I made all sorts of promises to God at the time – one of them being never to fly again.

What seemed like ages must have been about 30 minutes – the longest 30 minutes of my life! We finally landed at Lungi Airport. As we disembarked the hot sunshine hit me straight in my face. It seemed to envelop me in a warm embrace. The smell of the earth rose and the mix of rain and sunshine was soothing and welcoming. In a strange way I felt like I had come home. The children who had been excited and chattering away, suddenly clung to me and a silence took over. It was as if we were already in awe of this land – this strange but welcoming land. At that moment, corny as it may sound we fell in love with Africa; it was a feeling which was to tantalise and torment us in the future. But at that point I was content to be in the land of my husband's and children's heritage – a land which I fervently hoped would become 'home' to us!

Arriving at Lungi Airport did not mean the end of our journey. To get to Freetown people normally used a ferry.

Ferry from the airport in Sierra Leone

Winston's new employers were aware that Winston needed to be with his family – after sixteen years away it would have been insulting not to spend time with family. They had arranged for us to spend a weekend in Freetown before moving to the Mine in Yengema. We had a small aircraft at our disposal and it flew us to Hastings, which is just outside of Freetown. If I had been afraid of the flight from England to Sierra Leone, sitting in that small plane was indescribable. We could feel every judder and shudder – at times the ground seemed so visible that I thought we were going to crash. I sat on that plane with my heart in my mouth expecting the worst.

The only reassuring thing was the excitement of the children. This was all a major adventure and being in that small plane just put the icing on the cake. Even Paul seemed to have been caught up in the excitement and my heart lurched, seeing him desperately looking out of the tiny windows exclaiming at the sights below. There is something about the smell of Africa. To find the words to describe it is difficult – but it is a unique and unforgettable smell.

* * *

As Betty talked, my attention started to drift. A sense of nostalgia came over me. You see I was also born and lived in Africa and I knew what she meant. Although I came from the East and Betty was in the West, the vastness of the land had a certain fragility and dignity. I can never forget the smells after the rains – the earth seemed to swallow the water; the water soaked up the dry earth until we saw rivers of red mud. The sun, although fierce and as uncompromising as the land, was also enticing and embracing. To understand the beauty, majesty and power of Africa you had to have lived there and breathed the earth dust, vegetation and atmosphere deep into your lungs.

I heard Betty's calm voice in the distance and had to visibly shake myself to bring me to the present. It felt strange looking out of her front room window and seeing the daffodils and the watery grey skies! Betty seemed to instinctively know what I was feeling and gently said, "Shall we leave this for another time, love?"

We met up again a week later and Betty continued her story. "Where did I reach?" she asked me.

I told her about their arrival in Hastings. "Oh, yes...To get to Freetown we had to go by road..."

* * *

Although just outside Freetown, Hastings was a fair distance away. The journey to Freetown was a bumpy one. The rains had eroded some of the road away and there were massive potholes at various points. If we were not bouncing up and down in the car we were swaying left and right. The children thought this was great and got the giggles often. We pretended we were on safari and tried to spot any wild life around us.

Although the drive was a fair distance, time seemed to fly as we were caught up in all the newness around us. Even Winston seemed relaxed, treating our exclamations of surprise and wonder with a certain level of indulgence. At Freetown the car made its way to the Paramount Hotel. The plan was that we were to meet Bami at the hotel and he would take us to meet Winston's family.

It was nice to see Bami's familiar face as he welcomed us warmly. The children kept firing him lots of questions and he suggested having a drink at the hotel before making our way to the family. I was glad as it helped me get myself together a little. I was starting to feel very nervous with the thought of meeting Winston's family. It was now a reality and I did not know what to expect or even what they expected. I felt I could cope if Winston behaved himself but my experience did not make me confident about Winston's unpredictability. I think Bami must have sensed my nervousness as I was quite quiet and could not bring myself to ask my questions. Perhaps if I had I would have felt better, but when I was around Winston I always felt edgy and unsure of myself.

I was glad when we left the hotel to make our way to Winston's family home which was five minutes away. At least I could get over the first meeting and it would hopefully dispel some of my fears. You know it is strange how children can sense feelings – as we neared the house they clustered near me and Adele held onto my hand with fervour I had not experienced before. Winston's family lived on Pademba Road – I think the road was named after one of the local heroes. The house was built in a style which was referred to as a "Creole" house.

The family house Pademba Road

It was a wooden house, which had three stories and had a formidable air to it. Both the children and I were fascinated, as it was so different from the houses in Britain. Although the wood looked aged and tired it had a certain dignity about it. We went through a yard and entered through what seemed to be the back door.

As my eyes grew accustomed to the dimness it felt as if the room was crowded with people. It was only later that I found out that the extended family all lived there. Winston had of course not bothered to share details like this. As we stood in the middle of the room we were welcomed and told to sit down. I have never been so glad to see a chair! For some reason, I guess not being fully prepared about the climate, I was still in a wool suit that I had worn for the journey from England. It prickled and made me feel hot and uncomfortable and very English. The women around me wore flowing brightly coloured dresses and outfits and I know I must have looked so very odd. However no one made me feel strange and soon bottles of beer and soft drinks were brought.

Whilst we sipped our drinks, people filed past me to be introduced and shake to my hand. I guess this is the closest I would ever get to royalty! On meeting Winston's mother I knew it was her immediately. She was a beautiful woman who was very smart looking. Only her eyes had sadness about them. It was like looking into my eyes and I instinctively knew that this woman had experienced the same pain and rejection that I had. We could have been good friends but this was never to be so as circumstances took over. She also reminded me of Adele and meeting her for the first time I could imagine what my daughter would look like as an adult. I cannot remember the names of all the people I met but I particularly remember the warmth of a cousin of his. She was called Sissy George. I remember Sissy George because of a funny incident. Having had a drink I was desperate to go to the toilet. Sissy George took me. This was outside the main building and as I entered I saw lots of cockroaches. They were massive – I had seen cockroaches in England but not this size. Here I was, desperate to go to the loo, but terrified to do so because of these frightening creatures. Sissy George seemed to sense my fear and just smiled at me reassuringly. She then got hold of an empty tin and beat it hard with a stick making a dreadful noise and this made the cockroaches scuttle away. I have never used the loo so rapidly but was I glad that Sissy George was there!

At this point I had not met Winston's father and his two elder brothers. I found out that they had gone upstairs to discuss my presence and whether they would accept me as part of the family. To this day I do not know what the outcome of the meeting was; Winston said that there was a grudging acceptance particularly since I had had his children. What I did know was that it was customary for the men of the family to meet to discuss such issues particularly if the woman came from outside their particular tribe. Winston's family were Creole and tended to see themselves as elitist, so if they had rejected me it would have been because I was not Creole and not because I was white! I never warmed to Winston's father and two elder brothers and the children viewed them with some awe. Little did I know at the time that I would do battle with the patriarchs of the family – a battle which I was never to forget.

Throughout all this the children made friends with some of the children amongst us and were simply excited. I guess that getting grandparents, uncles, aunties and cousins must have been a wonderful experience – a sense of history being established. Just seeing the excitement in their faces and watching them rush around me made me feel warm. I felt that I had made the right decision to come to Sierra Leone – land of the lions – not for my sake, but the sake of my children. Whatever the future held for us they would forever have a sense of their heritage!

The arrangements for that weekend had been made for us. We were to stay with Bami and his wife Omo and their children. The family home was far too crowded and I did not argue with the arrangements, as the memory of the toilet was etched far too freshly in my mind.

After what seemed like a long time we said our goodbyes and made our way to Bami's house. I was relieved when we arrived at the house – it was a new and modern house, which belonged to the Bank he worked at. I know that I might sound snobbish and although I am very adaptable, I was just relieved that I could relax in a house which had some familiarity about it.

Bami and Omo lived in an area known as Wilberforce. The house was on a hill and from the verandah you got a spectacular view of the coastline and Freetown. That view was to give me much solace in the future. For the present I just sucked in the air and admired the view. Bami and Omo made us very welcome. They suggested we have a rest, shower and change for the evening. They had arranged for more family to come over.

We were to meet the Cummings; this was Winston's mother's side of the family. I knew that they were very wealthy, as Winston had often bragged about this. I was glad for the rest and the chance to get out of that uncomfortable wool suit.

Paul, Cris, Adele and Robert made friends with Bami and Omo's four children and seemed to be in their element. It was nice to hear their laughter and high-pitched tones as they were taken around the house and the garden.

We had a pleasant time that evening. I met Winston's cousins; Evlyn Cummings who was a doctor, Ronald who was a dentist in a place called Bo, and Evlyn's wife and family. Ronald was single at that time. They were all very warm and accepting of the children and me. It felt like real family and I felt sad as thoughts of my own family, particularly of my brother, crossed my mind.

Sitting in that room with the quiet of the night outside I realised what my children had been denied; I had always convinced myself that having me was enough, but listening to their laughter and chatter made me acknowledge the importance of kinship and family.

Omo who was heavily pregnant with her fifth child would not allow me to help or do a thing. She insisted on me relaxing and enjoying myself and I valued the opportunity to indulge myself. As soon as they saw us tiring they said their goodbyes and promised to meet up the next day. Was I glad to get to bed that night. It had been a long, tiring but exciting day.

As I lay in bed listening to Winston's snores I felt contented; although worried about the future. I had met some lovely people who were to become lifelong friends and havens of safety at times of need. For once I did not feel alone in the world – I somehow knew that these relatives of Winston would always be there for me. I must have drifted off to sleep at some point that night. It was a deep sleep and I was only awakened by the sound of the children's voices and the sun forcing light through the curtains.

It was Sunday, and I knew that the day had been planned for us and I was quite content to go along with the plans. Winston was being his charming self – acting the concerned and indulgent husband and father. Part of me knew this would not last, but I did not care. It was sufficient for the moment that he was not showing me up in front of his family and I had learned to make the most of moments like this.

As it was Sunday it was expected that we would accompany the family to church. I cannot really remember the denomination of the church but I think it was Methodist. It was a tradition to go to church and although both the children and I had not seen the inside of a church for a long time, it felt right to respect Bami and Omo's wishes and expectations.

We went to a church in Freetown and that was a new experience. I had never been in a church, or come to that, any other public place and seen so many black people. It was heart warming and although I got some questioning and inquisitive looks I really felt part of the congregation. A certain sense of peace came over me as I looked at each of my children – their faces were scrubbed and shiny, the boys looked serious and smart and Adele was as pretty as a picture, her eyes glistening with curiosity and excitement.

After the service I was introduced to some more people and we then made our way to the house of Evlyn and Ronald's father. He was an elder in the family and it was expected that we would visit and pay our respects. Again he was very welcoming – he was also a doctor. His wife embraced me warmly and formally welcomed me into the family.

My memory of that day was a round of visiting numerous relatives with food in abundance and everyone being warm and welcoming. I was left with little doubt of being accepted, my only doubt or should I say fear was Winston. But that could wait! That evening, sitting on the verandah sipping cold drinks, we seemed a million light years from the coldness and hostility of England. My children seemed to be blooming and everything felt right. We had an early night because the next day was an early start, as we would be flying to the Mine at Yengema.

Monday morning arrived. We got up early – the sun was a distant speck in the horizon. I was still getting used to the sudden dawns and dusks. There was nothing "gradual" in Africa. As usual I got the children ready without help from Winston. Omo gave us a good breakfast and Bami then dropped us off at the Paramount Hotel. The plan was that we were to be picked up from the hotel and flown into Yengema. I was dreading the flight, as I knew that it would be in a small plane similar to the one that brought us to Freetown.

We were picked up from the hotel and taken to the airfield at Hastings. By this time the children were wide-awake and were firing all sorts of questions. Who will meet us? Are there any children? Is it like the R.A.F? Is there a school near by? Questions I could not answer and ones that Winston avoided or answered in a vague way. I knew that he did not know what to expect but did not want to show his ignorance or nervousness – it would have been nice and reassuring if he had been able to show his human and unsure self!

Arriving at Hastings, my heart dropped when I saw the small plane. It looked so fragile and I could not believe that my children and I were to get into it as casually as getting into a car. There was another young couple with a baby waiting to board the same plane. This made me even more nervous, but I knew that this was not the time for hysterics, so I swallowed hard and boarded that plane. As usual the children thought this was a great adventure and couldn't contain their excitement. I had to insist on them putting on their safety belts and leaving them on. They sulked a little at first, but settled down once the plane started on the runaway. If I had not been so nervous the flight would have been a unique experience. It was still fairly early in the morning and as we flew into the clouds the morning mist was still visible. It was as if somebody had stroked the sky ever so gently and touched it with a paintbrush dipped in pink candy floss. At that time you could feel the Harmattan – a cool wind from the Sahara – as it gently rocked the plane from side to side.

We were not flying very high and the people and houses on the ground were still visible. The children were enthralled with this and Robert was convinced that he was flying over Toyland – he kept asking Winston to stop the plane so that he could visit Toyland! One moment we were all caught up with the experience and the next moment looking up, I saw a huge hill looming in front. The first time that this happened I shrieked in terror and everybody thought this was really funny. But the plane casually tilted at an angle and flew over the hill before settling down to a level flight.

It took us about an hour of hills, flatness and the Harmattan to get to Yengema. By this time I was fairly fatalistic and had stopped worrying but was glad to feel terra firma again! From Yengema we were driven to the Mine. There Winston's cousin Ivor was waiting for us. Ivor was the half brother of Evelyn and Ronald. His mother was white and he was of mixed parentage. This was comforting to me and I wondered why Winston had not told me this. It would have been reassuring to know that I was not the first white woman in the family – even if it was on his mother's side.

Ivor was one of the directors at the Mine and had clearly used his influence to get Winston the job. He had other personnel from the Mine with him and after welcoming us, he took us to the house where we would be living.

It became clear that Ivor had gone through a lot of trouble to make us welcome. The house was comfortable and was stocked up with food. He left us there to relax and said he would return at "sundown" to familiarise us with the place and arrangements. Although the flight had only been for an hour it felt that we were light years away from Freetown. The ruggedness of the land stared at us through each window and England seemed dreamlike. It felt lonely and I wondered if I would make friends and whether the children would be able to attend local schools. However I put the questions to the back of my mind, determined to ask Ivor later, but in the meantime started unpacking and making us comfortable in what would be our home for the foreseeable future.

When Ivor came round that evening he seemed to instinctively know my questions. He told us that he had arranged for Paul and Cris to attend boarding school at a place called Bo. This was half way between Freetown and Yengema about 150 miles away. Bo sounded familiar to me and Winston reminded me that this was where Ronald had his dental practice. Ivor told me it was a grammar school and the new term was just beginning so it would be good for the boys to start school soon. My heart dropped – Paul and Cris were only about thirteen and twelve, and they had never been away from me for any long period of time.

My heart dropped even further when I was told that Adele would also be going as a boarder to a school in an area called Brookfields – Freetown Secondary School for Girls. I did not know what to say as I realised that Ivor had gone through a lot of trouble organising this. I had also expected that schools would involve distance but not in my wildest dreams had I imagined that the children would be living away from me. I asked in a feeble voice whether there were local schools and Winston gave me an angry stare. But I had to ask! Ivor tried to reassure me that Robert would be attending a local school and that it was customary for children to be sent as boarders to school – it was important that the children got a good education.

I felt real anger at Winston; why had he not prepared me – perhaps he had been afraid that I would not have accompanied him to Africa. But I should have been told; I could have prepared the children. Their quiet faces just stared at me as if expecting me to change things. I could only look at them helplessly. Cris kept pleading with me saying he would be good and look after Robert if only he could stay, Paul had withdrawn into himself and Adele bravely tried to hold her tears back as she looked at me accusingly. It was as clear as crystal that we had no alternatives – my three children would have to go to boarding school, and I would have to live with the memory of their faces etched in my mind. I tried to explain but simply could not find the words to make them feel better – after all I was having difficulty coping with the thought of the enforced separation.

All the time Winston had known about the arrangements and had deliberately chosen not to say anything to us! That first night in Yengema must have been the longest night in our lives – this might sound like an exaggeration but that is how it felt. Robert was the only one who had not fully realised the significance of his brothers and sister going away to school. Paul had gone very quiet and was almost sullen. It did not help that I could not give them any sense of where they were going and Winston just said he did not want to be troubled and the children were my responsibility.

As he lay beside me snoring away, I felt a deep sense of hatred for this man; his thoughtlessness and cruelty seemed to have no boundaries. Paul and Cris were to have only a few days with me before they went off to their school. Adele was to have about four weeks before she needed to start school.

I had a hundred and one things to do so that they were ready for school. I had to sort out school uniforms, things like mosquito nets and bed linen. All this needed to be put in separate boxes ready to be transported to the school. Time seemed to fly and it was soon time for me to take the boys to their new school at Bo.

All the way to Bo, Paul was very quiet and I knew that he was angry with me. Cris just kept on like a broken record saying that he did not want to go and that he would run away. I tried convincing them that they would be okay and that time would fly and we would be together during the holidays, but I knew that they were not reassured. I also had to convince myself that this was for the best. Ivor had told me that the school had an excellent reputation and that a lot of chiefs and people in high places sent their children there. At least they would get a good education and they would adjust to their new environment.

Deep down I knew that I was only fooling myself; it felt wrong that I could not be with them during this traumatic time. They were already trying to adjust to the climate, food and style of life and now I was expecting them to adjust to being away from the only familiar people they knew. I really felt bad but dared not show my true feelings.

When we got to the school at Bo I noticed that the hospital was next door. This is where Ronald worked as a dentist. I felt a sense of relief and took the boys over to say hello. I guess I was hoping that this would reassure them. Ronald was warm and welcoming and promised to keep an eye on the boys and told them that he would come and take them out regularly. I could see from their faces that they were determined not to respond to this. Part of me wanted to shout at them and tell them that it was their father's fault. It was breaking my heart to see them so unhappy but I was a stranger in this land and dependent on the wisdom and goodwill of others. But I did not say a word. We said our goodbyes to Ronald and made our way to the school.

The headmaster seemed a little stern but was welcoming. He showed us the boys' dormitory and reassured me that they would be all right once they had made friends. However my heart sank a little when he made it clear that the boys had to eat at the school and could not go to relatives on weekdays. This would only be allowed over school holidays. I knew that this was not going to work but dared not say it, so I just said my goodbyes, kissed and hugged the children and left not daring to look at their tearful faces.

I felt very bitter – I had never envisaged travelling all this way only to be separated from my two boys. I could not forgive myself as I felt that I had let them down and knew no way to make it better!

On getting back to Yengema the house seemed empty. Although Adele and Robert were there they were not their usual exuberant selves. The African adventure had turned sour.

Winston did not even bother to ask after the boys. I just tried to settle down to getting Adele ready for school and making that house a little like home. Every day for the next two weeks I got a letter from Paul and Cris saying how unhappy they were and that they wanted to come home. I felt as if I had deserted them even if it was not my fault. I should have stood up to Winston and insisted that he sorted out another more appropriate school. I could not talk to him and I had no one to share my feelings with – I felt so alone.

It must have been about two and a half weeks later that we received a telegram from the head teacher. He asked us to come and get the boys as they were refusing to eat and he did not want the responsibility any longer. He suggested a day school as more appropriate. Winston was furious and blamed me for mollycoddling the children – he would make men of them! Let them starve - they would have to give in some time.

At this point I put my foot down and said we had to go to the school and try and sort things out, and if necessary move the boys. As expected Winston took no responsibility and said that it had nothing to do with him and he was not going to arrange transport in the plane. If I wanted to go to Bo I would have to go by car! I did not want to argue with him so I got Ivor to arrange a car and travelled by road to Bo. It was a long and dusty journey – it was a lot of road for Africa.

To get to Bo we had to drive through Kenema. This was where Evlyn had his surgery. The people in the area spoke English and or Creole. It was easy to get directions to his surgery, as he was the only doctor in the area. It was good to see his familiar face again. He insisted on me having something to eat and having a drink of tea. I was relieved to relax in a chair that did not move and caught up with some of the family gossip. We must have stopped for an hour before I decided it was time to continue the journey to Bo. When I eventually arrived in Bo I asked the driver to take me to the hospital first. At the hospital I was fortunately able to see Ronald and asked him if he could accompany me to the headmaster. He was very kind and agreed to do so. It should have been Winston and I felt a certain sense of shame that I had to ask his cousin, who was virtually a stranger to me.

The headmaster was very firm and inflexible. He would not hear of agreeing to the boys eating at Ronald's. I tried to explain that this was a new experience to them; living away from their family, getting used to a different culture, climate and food. But he was adamant that the boys had to go – he could not make exceptions. If he agreed to them eating at Ronald's he would be inundated with all sorts of demands from the other children, and that would be the end of discipline. He was so pompous that I wanted to throttle him. But I controlled myself and agreed to take the boys back with me.

Paul and Cris were overjoyed to see me and as I hugged and kissed them I could see that they had lost weight. I knew that I had made the right decision. Both Ronald and the driver helped us to load the car and we made our way back to Yengema. The journey took us two days with a break at Evlyn's in Kenema. All the way the boys' faces looked so relieved that I did not have the heart to tell them off. Instead throughout that journey I just imagined Winston's reaction – I knew that he would be furious. God alone knew what he would do to me, but for the moment I was glad to have my two boys back with me!

When we arrived back at Yengema I was relieved that Winston was not home. Adele and Robert were there with the houseboy that Ivor had employed on our behalf. I got Paul and Cris to go to their room and to keep out of sight when Winston returned home. This was difficult as Robert and Adele were so excited to see their big brothers that they would not leave them alone. Winston came home about six o'clock that evening. I could hear the children chattering and knew that he had heard them as well. He went livid and started yelling at me, slapping me across my face. The children had gone very quiet in the next room and I knew that they had heard the crack of his hand across my face. With my cheek burning I tried to keep calm and to explain that I had no alternative but to bring them home. I then made the mistake of mentioning that Ronald had come with me and had agreed with the decision to bring the boys home. Foolishly I had thought that this would make things better - at least he would know that I had consulted a member of his family. How wrong could I be! He went berserk and started calling me awful names ... saying that I was trying to show him up in front of his family... he grabbed hold of me by the shoulders and shook me until I could not breathe... I felt like a rag doll – as I started feeling faint he suddenly pushed me away and I fell to the ground....he casually stepped over me and told me that he wanted nothing to do with any school arrangements and that he would be out for the night. I did not know where he was going and I did not care.

As I picked myself off the floor, I wearily went to the kitchen to get the children's evening meal ready. As I passed their bedroom they crept out quietly. Paul came to put his arms round me – it hurt... but I put on my "cheerful" face, reassured them that I was all right and got them to help me with the meal.

That night when the children were in bed I sat in the living room looking out at the African night. It was pitch black and I could see a few stars in the sky, but they seemed a long long way away. I felt weary – what was I to do about schools? I dared not consult Ivor or even Bami as I was afraid of Winston's reaction. He always wanted to let others believe that he was a caring and considerate father and that I was the problem.

Much as I had fallen in love with Africa, I wished that I was back in England – at least there I knew my way about and had some control over the children and my environment. Here in Yengema I was utterly and completely at the mercy of Winston and his family! The time had come to take Adele to her school in Freetown. It was only a couple of days since Paul and Cris had come home. I had given the matter some thought and had decided to try the grammar school in Freetown for the boys. Although not very sure whether it was a day and/or boarding school I thought that I would take a chance. If it was only a day school, I would be stuck as I really did not want the boys to stay with the family in Pademba Road, but I decided to face this if it became a reality.

Adele was packed and ready. She was very quiet and did not create a scene. I was grateful for this but also took her silence for granted.

I never thought that the row with Winston was still fresh in the children's mind and that they would go along with any plans just to keep me safe. I must have appeared so selfish and heartless... but I was just grateful for their acquiescence!

Ivor had sorted out the plane for us. I was to take Paul, Cris and Adele with me. Robert was to stay behind with our houseboy who also was a friend to me and the children. He agreed to look after Robert whilst I was away and I knew that he could be trusted.

I have little memory of that flight to Freetown – in some way the excitement had been knocked out of us. We might be in a new country but we all knew that our experiences of being a family were to remain the same – fearful and living on our nerves.

When we got to Freetown there was a company bus waiting to take us to Bami and Omo's house. It was great to see them again. The children's faces also lit up as Bami warmly welcomed us. This was to become a familiar pattern to our visits to Freetown. There was no formality; we could just turn up and we would be welcomed unreservedly. It did not matter how long we stayed.... we were encouraged to treat their house as our home. This was all so different from England... where you simply would not dream of turning up on someone else's doorstep without prior warning!

Being with Bami and Omo was a relief. At least it was temporary refuge from Winston and the loneliness of Yengema. The next day we went to pay our respects to Winston's father and mother. His mother embraced us warmly but his father maintained a distance. After staying there for a couple of hours we made our way to Adele's new school to meet with the head teacher. I could sense that Adele was not happy but did not dare encourage her to say this to me. She was very quiet and I knew that this was her way of coping. My head was so full of the boys and needing to find a school for them that I gave Adele little thought. I was just relieved that she was not making a fuss. At the school we met the head teacher who struck me as a bit of a cold fish. I did not warm to her and was a little concerned on the emphasis on obedience and rules. But I also knew that this was a good school so I put my anxieties aside. She agreed to Adele coming in from Bami's until I returned to Yengema; Adele would then move in as a boarder. I was happy about this arrangement and could see from Adele's little face that she was pleased. We now had to sort out the boys.

That evening I talked to Bami about possibilities. I was aware that if Winston found out that I had consulted with Bami his wrath would have no boundaries. But I had to talk to someone even if Winston disapproved. He encouraged me to try the Grammar school, as both Winston and he were ex-students. He knew the head teacher who was a neighbour and was sure that he would help even though the school term had started. The only problem was accommodation but this could be dealt with later.

Bami insisted on contacting the head teacher, a Mr. Woods, and arranged for me to see him the next day. It felt such a relief to have someone that I could rely on; I can never forget the warmth and kindness of Bami and Omo, and the unquestioning acceptance of myself who really was a stranger to them. Little did they know, they were to be my refuge and my strength in Africa.

* * *

My next meeting with Betty took place after a three-week break. During this time Betty had been admitted to hospital and had been very ill. When I met up with her again, Africa seemed a lifetime away. She looked pale and tired and by now I knew Betty well enough to realise she was in a lot of pain. However although the person sitting across from me looked frail and grey.... I could only see beyond the greyness.

What I saw was a woman of enormous strength.... a woman who carried around with her a heavy brown paper parcel labelled GUILT ...a woman who felt she had let down the most important people in her life – her children... a woman who fought to survive, determined to tell her story – however painful... a legacy to leave to her children and her children's children.

Fragile though she looked, Betty was like a wild daisy...on the outside she looked like any other woman of her age... but if you looked closer and looked beyond the common white and yellow of the daisy, you saw that each petal was unique...the centre yellowness although similar was different...no two flowers were exactly alike... the outer appearance was there to test... to see whether we saw beyond the white and yellow... and like the daisy many attempts were made to uproot it, but these attempts were not successful....her roots were firmly embedded in the soil... clinging on determinedly... facing all weathers, all weed killers, all attempts to destroy it ... but clinging on, determined to let go only when she was ready. Yes, I had learnt to look beyond the obvious -– beyond the fragility.

Betty could not remember where we had stopped, so I told her.

She smiled at me and said, "This story is resurrecting demons that I had thought I had laid to rest. Whilst in hospital I remembered how I was in Africa. And I had to smile to myself, as I saw myself as a young woman again, a woman in her thirties/or was it late twenties? You know I must have cut a very strange figure out there in Africa. I was very stylish and always liked to dress smartly. Never mind appropriately, smart and fashionable was important. It was as if my outside could hide the vulnerability on the inside of me. Walking around in Freetown, Yengema in my stilettos and straight skirts I must have looked silly. But I did not care; I had to look confident and cocky – no one should really guess the truth of my soft centre. And you know, I was always getting things wrong – I tried my best, but it was as if my best was not good enough!

"I can remember one incident. There was a funeral of a close family friend, Winston's family I mean. Not knowing otherwise I wore black, thinking it was a sign of respect. I had got it all wrong, particularly since I was the only person in black; everyone was in blue and yellow. I can see myself as clearly as it was yesterday – standing in church with my ridiculous shoes and black outfit. Winston had not bothered to tell me that people did not always wear black. The deceased or their family would inform mourners what colour should be worn at the funeral. There was I, the English woman, in her black dress and her stiletto shoes! I was always in trouble for getting things wrong.

"Winston in a perverse way enjoyed my humiliation – although he would have a go at me he never told me what was appropriate and correct; he just let me get it wrong. I guess it gave him the excuse to ridicule me but it is only now that I realise that this suited him. By getting it wrong, everybody could believe I was this disrespectful white woman, this feather-brain. It gave Winston the permission to treat me like dirt and to continue his philandering ways. I always got it wrong... so wrong."

* * *

To get back to where we had stopped last. It was so important that I sorted out the boys' school. I had an appointment with the Principal of the Grammar school. Bami had arranged this, as the man was a neighbour of his. I dressed in my smartest outfit and with my stilettos and the boys I made my way to meet with the Principal, Mr. Woods.

Meeting Mr. Woods was a surprise, as he turned out to be an Englishman. I do not know why I was surprised, but I was! He was very sympathetic and patiently listened to me. I explained what had happened and that I was desperate to get my sons into a good school. I told him that both Winston and Bami were ex-students, hoping that this would help. Mr. Woods was ever so nice but he did not fully appreciate my sense of relief when he agreed to have the boys. He said that the term had started but he would make space for the boys even if he had to buy new desks to accommodate them. The only snag was that they would be day students. However, at that point, I only felt an overwhelming sense of relief that I had got Paul and Cris into a good school – one which Winston could not fault.

That night I was sitting on the verandah of Bami's house. Throughout the day and at that point I was tussling with the idea of accommodation for the boys. I knew that Winston would never agree to me getting a house in Freetown, he would claim that I was showing him up. Bami's house would be ideal but I did not want to take advantage of their kindness. The only possibility was the family at Pademba Road – I was sure that Winston's mother would look after them, but I did not know how the boys would cope. There were a hundred and one little things that would be different... things as basic as being used to running water and the privacy of a bathroom... at Pademba road they would have to wash in the open courtyard... what the heck was I to do?

I was so engrossed in my thoughts that I did not hear Bami join me. He gave me a start when he said, "You are worried about the boys, aren't you?" All I could do was nod...

"Do not worry, Betty, they can stay here with me and Omo. We will look after them. So please don't worry."

I wanted to say, "No, I cannot ask this of you... " but the words would not come out as a sense of relief gushed over me – it was like the gush of water when a dam breaks. I was just so, so relieved and all I could do was thank him with all my heart. The boys were so pleased – they got on well with Bami's children and would be accompanying his eldest son to school every day.

Seeing their happy faces made me feel that the right decision was made – but you know, I was so focused on the boys that I completely forgot about Adele. I must have seemed so callous to her... putting her in a boarding school and then making special arrangements for Paul and Cris. I never even asked her how she felt – I just made a whole lot of assumptions.

Little did I know at the time that Bami was going to be a loving figure in my children's lives. I also did not know that his eldest son was to die as a child – he drowned at Lumley Beach. Paul and Cris were devastated at the loss of their friend.

I also had assumed that Winston would make arrangements to pay for Paul and Cris's upkeep – but I am pretty sure that he never did. At the time I was only glad that I could safely leave my children in Freetown knowing that there would be someone I trusted looking out for them.

Even leaving a tearful Adele at her school before returning to Yengema, I still failed to see the pain and hurt in my daughter's eyes. All I could see and feel was a sense of relief... relief that I would not have to face Winston's wrath, relief that I had at last got something right in his eyes and the eyes of his family. Adele my beautiful daughter, who tried to protect me with her silence. The only girl amongst three boys, you would think that she would have been cosseted and spoilt. The truth is that she often missed out as she always tried to be as much part of the surroundings as she could.

The children were all afraid of Winston and besides Paul, who often confronted him, they learnt very quickly to avoid him. Adele most of all. It was this that made it easy to ignore her pain and confusion. I always consoled myself with the fact that I did my best... I did everything I humanly could, but somewhere deep down I felt that I had failed this tall, brown-eyed daughter of mine. It was sending her to Freetown School for Girls which really brought this home for me. My concern was to give the children a good education – more so for Adele. I was determined that my daughter would not end up like me – she would be independent and free to make choices, without being tied to a man. So I was taken in by the school's reputation. I never knew the full truth of her experience in that school. Why? I never asked. I was so caught up in my world, in Winston... that I never asked. I only found out the truth much later. Adele had been desperately unhappy at school.

Although the school had a good reputation it was a hard school. Discipline was rigid and applied through the use of a cane. Hitting the girls to get them to conform was the accepted norm. Adele also faced a lot of bullying and taunting by the other girls. This was because she spoke and looked different. She hated the school but she never told me and I never asked. She knew that I had to return to Yengema and never understood why she had to sleep at school and the boys lived with Uncle Bami. And I never bothered to explain. I was so full of guilt at being so far away and only able to visit when the school decreed it okay... and also when the plane at Yengema was available... I never explained how it really was.

Bami must have been some kind of refuge for her; maybe he was there for her when I wasn't. All I know is that she has always had a lot of time for Bami and his family. I know that Adele carries with her a lot of feelings about her time in Freetown and her time at that school. I often look at Adele, her supple and lithe body so much like me in so many ways... I look into her liquid brown eyes, always so busy... and I see pain ... deep pools of pain hidden so deep that I can only see it; I carry with me the pain of knowing that I never asked.

Back at Yengema life with Winston was no different; I could have been in any country and things would not change. I missed Paul, Cris and Adele. I know that Robert missed them too – the house was quiet and the sounds of children's voices did not echo within its walls. But I was glad to have Robert with me. He was at the age where he did not mind being babied but he also wanted to be treated as a young man. And his questions, I have never heard a child ask so many "Why's". In some way without needing to vie for my attention with the older children, he became more confident and secure. We had some good times together although we both missed the others –Paul, Cris and Adele. As to Winston, he came and went as he pleased, and always expected me to be the dutiful wife.

It must have been a couple of weeks before I sensed something was wrong. You would have thought that by this time I would be an expert in detecting when he was up to his old tricks. Not me; the ever-trusting and gullible fool that I was. I first noticed that when I went to the local shops people would stare at me and start whispering. Initially I thought it was just because I was a stranger in their midst. But when people started avoiding me I knew that something was badly wrong. I confronted Winston and asked him what was going on. He just casually brushed my demands aside and said that some of the men were jealous of him and were spreading rumours that he was stealing from the Mine. I instinctively knew that he was lying. But rather than make him angry, I decided to pretend to believe him. Like all things the truth came home to roost soon after.

Ivor came over to the house and looked both grim and furious. Winston wanted me to make myself scarce but I knew that there was real trouble brewing, so I insisted on staying. Robert was in his bedroom doing his schoolwork. I had never seen or heard Ivor being so angry. It seemed that Winston had been borrowing his friend, Abdul's, van. He had been stealing tyres from the Mine and transporting them in the van. They had tried to catch him at it but he somehow always managed to get away with it. Winston tried to sweet talk Ivor, saying that this was all lies and that people were trying to frame him, particularly because they knew he was a cousin of the "boss". He sounded so plausible that I almost wanted to believe him. Ivor was having none of this. It was clear that he did not believe a word. He told Winston that the only reason that the police had not been called out was because of Ivor's position in the company. Winston had to resign or he would be sacked. Ivor said that Winston needed to keep the good name of the family and he had better resign or things would get heavy. I sat through this in silence feeling a sense of deja vu. The same old tune; the same old song...

Reluctantly Winston agreed to resign. Ivor suggested he move to Tongofield and finish his notice there. I was starting to feel really angry – I was starting to feel settled and once again I had to move, and it was all because of Winston. I did not have a clue where Tongofield was and I wanted to ask Ivor to let me stay on in the house. But I knew from the glitter in Winston's eyes to keep my mouth shut.

That evening all hell broke loose and I was subjected to a tirade of abuse. As usual I was to blame... How? Don't ask me... it just gave him the excuse to use me as his "whipping boy". Fed up and sick to my teeth I started packing, getting our things together; why did I ever bother to unpack? Once I had got over the shock of what had happened and stopped packing like a robot, I gave the move some thought. Winston was being really nice and was full of apologies; still maintaining that he had been framed. I did not believe him but could not be bothered to say so. I went along with his charade. So when he suggested thta he would move first to Tongofield and sort out accommodation, I agreed. It made sense ... and it would give me more time to sort out the packing.

Winston left in a couple of days and I followed a few weeks later. Winston had been employed at the Mine on the basis of local conditions and not on overseas terms. I knew that he had always resented this and felt that the Mine was exploiting him. My understanding of employment conditions was limited so I never really knew whether he had legitimate grounds to feel aggrieved. Whatever the case this did not make it all right to steal from his employers. I told him that he needed to behave himself at Tongofield, as he needed a decent reference if he was to get another job. He was contrite and promised to behave himself, actually he said "he would have to watch his back." which I guess is quite different.

When he left for Tongofield we seemed to be on better terms with each other and I actually thought things were taking an upward turn. More fool I! My nightmare was to begin. At Yengema the shops refused to provide me with goods and food. I was shocked to find out that he had told the shops to stop supplying me with goods. I felt so humiliated but also worried as to how I was to feed Robert and myself. What could I do? Just when I was at the point of deciding to go to Tongofield and turn up on his doorstep, one of the bosses at the Mine came to see me. He told me that he had heard through the grapevine that I was left with no food. I have never felt so embarrassed and was grateful that he was not Ivor. He had made contact with the shops and had overruled Winston's decision. He had made arrangements that some of Winston's wages would come directly to me; in this way I would be able to look after my children and myself. At the time I felt an overwhelming sense of relief. This seemed to take over any embarrassment I had felt – at least I now had a means of supporting Robert and myself. But I also knew that Winston would be furious and see this as me "showing him up". I was going to have to pay for this, but for the moment I was independent of him and felt a real sense of release.

When I finally joined him at Tongofield, he did not even bother to come and meet us. We had to find our own way to the house. I felt as if there was a large fist in a glove around my heart. This fist kept squeezing, first ever so gently, and then harder and harder, until I felt that I could not breathe. This fear was because I knew that a confrontation was waiting for me!

He turned up that evening, and just looked at me as if I was a piece of dirt stuck to his shoe. I tried to pretend that I did not notice the anger swirling around and calmly asked him if he had his tea. He then flipped and started shouting at me calling me foul names. As he came near I could feel his hot breath, I felt as if he was scorching me the words and abuse just kept on coming; it was like being caught up in a river during the rains... the water swollen, beating itself against me... knowing that I could not fight against the tide... finally giving up... just waiting to see if I drowned or survived.... and when it felt that it would not stop, he pushed me aside and I lost my footing and fell. He shoved me with his foot, stepped over me, put food on his plate and ate without a word. When he finished he left his plate on the table and walked out of the house. He did not come back that night and I did not care.

The time spent in Tongofield was to be even more humiliating and painful than at Yengema. In Tongofield Winston had been given the responsibility to let and manage houses owned by the Mine. I found out through the usual whispers that he was housing the different women that he was having affairs with. Whilst I was there he had three different women on the go, two of them prostitutes. He did not bother to be discrete and seemed to enjoy throwing this in my face. What was even more painful was that one of the women was the woman who had first travelled with us on the flight to Yengema. She had had a young baby with her and in Yengema I had befriended her, often helping her out with the baby. I happened to bump into her at the local shop in Tongofield and expressed surprise to see her. She told me that she had come to visit her father. I invited her over to our house but she never took up the invitation. At the time I thought she was behaving oddly but did not think anything of it. It was only later that I found out that she had been having an affair with Winston and was in Tongofield to see him. I felt so cheated and a deep sense of hurt.

I was pretty sure that Winston must have been stealing from the Company that he worked for, as I knew that his wages would not cover the upkeep of these women. Never have I been so grateful to know that I did not have to go to him for money. I was still receiving a portion of his wages directly and used that for the upkeep of the children and myself. It was not much but it kept the wolf from the door and gave me a certain level of independence.

The time spent both at Yengema and Tongofield was a painful and unhappy time. Here was I, a stranger in a breathtaking land, isolated and alone, constantly pitied by outsiders and humiliated by my husband. You would have thought that with all his women Winston would have no interest in me. On the contrary, he expected me to perform so called "wifely" duties. I cannot remember the number of times he assaulted or raped me during this period. There was a mass of confusion in my head, because he could be tender and gentle one moment and violent the next. I did not dare say anything to anyone as I felt responsible. Some days I did not want to wake up and just prayed for the fist in the glove to squeeze life out of me but then I would think of the children, Paul, Cris, Adele and Robert so innocent in the next room and knew that I could not stop breathing. I had to live, if only to protect the children from their father and my husband. The marriage vows often danced mockingly in my head 'to have and to hold' 'to honour...' hollow words which seemed a lifetime away...

It was now time to return to Freetown. Winston had completed his notice and the plans were to return. He would stand a much better chance of getting another job there. I was relieved to leave the isolation of Tongofield for the bustle of Freetown. At least I knew people there and had made some good friends through Bami and Omo. Although I knew that this would not be a fresh start, I hoped that the close presence of family and friends would put some pressure on Winston to behave. Deep down I knew that this was nonsense but I had to hold onto something to make our lives more bearable. There was no escape – Africa was a long way from England – and I was not even sure whether I wanted to return to that cold and unforgiving land.

Our relationship had gone from bad to worse – he did not even bother hiding his indiscretions. I often found letters from women, sometimes items of clothing and people were talking openly about him. I knew that he would have to give up his women friends in Tongofield – I just hoped, desperately, he would behave or at least not be so brazen about his infidelity. The children were now at an age where they would be able to pick up gossip and understand it; they had a fair idea as to what their father was capable of. It was bad enough that I was humiliated and pitied; I simply wanted to protect them and help them hold onto their self respect. So I was glad to be returning to Freetown.

The move to Freetown was hectic; Winston did not help. Again, the rigmarole of packing, sorting out unpaid bills, and saying our farewells. In Sierra Leone at that time, if you did not work there was no money coming in; there was no welfare, you are basically on your own. Until Winston got a job we would have no money to support us. I used to keep aside and quietly save some of the money that I received from his wages, but I did not tell him about this – I had put it aside for the children.

In Freetown the plan was that Winston, Paul and Cris would live at Pademba Road with his family. Adele, Robert and I were to stay with Bami and Omo. On the one hand the arrangements were a relief but I despaired for Paul and Cris. I wanted all the children with me, but the practicality of accommodating all of us was an impossibility, and Winston insisted on the two oldest being with him. Not because he cared but just to present to the world that he was a considerate and caring husband and father. Paul promised to look after Cris and I said that I would see them everyday and this was only a short-term arrangement. I knew that they were not happy and wanted to be with me, but they made a minimum of fuss, I guess to protect me. I was happy to have all the children close by and Adele's relief to become a day pupil made me feel that I had made the right decision as a short-term measure.

The thought of having to pack and unpack made me decide that we would live from our suitcases. It would also help us believe that this was a temporary arrangement. I was in the process of sorting out Winston's things when I found a letter in one of his shirt pockets. To this day I do not know whether he had deliberately left it there, knowing that I would find it, or whether it was an accident. I was devastated by the contents of the letter but was determined that I would give Winston no sign that I had found it. I hid it and behaved as if nothing had happened – although inside I was a mass of churning emotions. There seemed to be no depths too low for this man, my husband, would sink to!

That evening with Winston, Paul and Cris back at his parents' house and Adele and Robert in bed, I was on the verandah at Bami's house. You know I loved that verandah – it was all so peaceful you could smell Freetown; the distant lights always gave it a fairy like appearance. If I had any thoughts of heaven, this is what heaven would be like. The darkness of the African night, the sounds of the crickets and the steaming smell of the land was soothing – it helped me think.

In the dim light of the verandah I read that letter again. It was from one of his women friends. She wrote about her relationship with him and said she would love to have a child with him; the way it was written it seemed as if the idea of having a child came from Winston however the only way she would have a child was if he got rid of me. The letter sickened me – he could not even look after his own children and he was talking of having another child and what did "get rid of her" mean? My mind just went into hysterical overdrive. I just sat there with tears rolling down my face. I made no sound... no sound could pass my lips I just felt this tearing within me. I thought that I knew what Winston was capable of but I did not! What I had to acknowledge was that deep inside of me, a part of me did love this man – that is why he could hurt me – I was deeply ashamed that I still could love a man who abused my children and humiliated me. What was wrong with me?

Bami had come to look for me. As he called out my name I hastily averted my head trying to wipe my cheeks discretely. He must have seen the tears because he asked me what was wrong. I could not speak. I dared not speak in case I made a complete fool of myself. I silently gave him the letter to read. It felt as if the silence was wrapping us in a warm cloak, insulating me from further pain he gave the letter back to me, and said, "Betty I am so sorry, so sorry..." then the tears came like a river in flood, my body shaking as if I was a leaf in a thunderstorm. The fist in the glove around my heart squeezed and squeezed until I started gasping... this kind man said not a word; he just let the pain take over but his presence comforted me, for I knew that I had found a friend for life. You know the old saying, "the devil looks after his own" – well, this always seemed to be the case with Winston. It did not seem to matter as to what he had done, or was capable of doing, he always landed on his feet.

It was not long before he got an offer of a job. It was with a cement company owned by Israelis. Despite his employment record, he always managed to get good jobs. In some way this was reassuring as it meant others were taken in by his charm – so I forgive myself for being a gullible fool.

Winston was appointed as a Manager in charge of wages. When he told me this, I had to try and stop myself from smiling. Wasn't it ironic? I wouldn't trust him with my life let alone money – and here he was, with an accessible bank account and unlimited access to someone else's money!

He decided to rent a house from one of his cousins. It was in an area known as Banana Water. I was not consulted but told; he needed a nice house because he was expected to entertain clients and colleagues. When I saw the house I fell in love with it immediately. It was a beautiful house with two floors. The living accommodation was on the second floor and the first floor had the kitchen and place for drying our clothes when it rained. There was lots of space for the children to play, although we were warned about snakes. It just meant that they would have to be careful and always wear shoes if they were outside.

Despite the best intentions, outside without shoes, Banana Water Rd

Bami tried to persuade me against moving – he thought it was a bad idea and would make me vulnerable to Winston's temper and moods. But I had to move – I owed it to Paul and Cris. I wanted my children to be together again – we needed to be like family – we only had each other. I was prepared to sacrifice anything as long as we were together and I could ensure the relative safety of my children. Somehow I had to make it work – if this was the only way I could have all my children with me, then so be it. I would make it work.

The move to Banana Water was conducted with the minimum of fuss. Most of our things were still in packing cases so I did not have to do a lot of packing. Winston had started work so the move was left to me. The children were all in school so I could get on with the task. I had a young man to help me move any heavy stuff. I remember in the midst of unpacking I had this desperate thirst for a cup of tea. Nothing else would do, but I had no hot water. The young man told me to wait and went to the house across the road. As I stood in the doorway wondering what he was up to, this woman came out of the house towards me with a tray of tea and biscuits. This was the way it is in Africa – people have time for you, hospitality is essential. The woman introduced herself as Valerie. After joining me in finishing the tea and biscuits, she stayed for a while and helped me, giving me all the gossip of the area. I found out that she was a Jehovah Witness but she never ever preached her religion to me.

Valerie was to become a good friend; during some of my worst moments, she was always there for me to talk to. I knew that I could trust her and what I told her would not be a source of gossip.

She never acted as if she was sorry for me, she respected me and I valued this. She was just there for me – no questions asked, no expectations of me. All of which made me feel good.

We settled down pretty quickly at Banana Water. The children were pleased to be together again and outwardly we were able to mimic life in an ordinary family. Winston and I had very little to do with each other – he would expect food and sex... in that order... and I went through the motions of being the dutiful wife. If this meant that it gave the children and me some semblance of normality, then it was a price worth paying.

As a manager, Winston was expected to entertain people like Captains and their wives from the ships bringing in cement; and other personnel. I obviously was expected to do the catering and quite enjoyed doing this. It was a diversion and helped me use my energy up. Many a night we would hold a dinner party where we both got in role, me the dutiful wife, and Winston the hard working husband. What a charade! I used to sometimes sit there wondering what people would say if I told them the truth about our relationship – about the real rotting stench of abuse and violence – and while these thoughts whirled around in my head, I would smile and talk as if I had not a care in the world.

Winston opened an account for me in a shop in the town. This meant I could get what I needed without having to ask him. I was grateful for this small mercy. I knew that he was seeing other women and was not faithful to me. But I couldn't do anything about it. He had access to a car and a driver but I had to walk or use the bus. It hurt to see and know that his other women had use of the car but again there was little that I could do about it. I constantly used to ask myself what was I doing wrong... was it something about me... did I have a large neon sign over my head saying "VICTIM"– why me? Although Winston's behaviour hurt me terribly I had learned not to show my hurt – I had become just as good an actress as he was an actor!

We must have been living in Banana Water for about three or four months when the facade of being an ordinary family started to seriously crack. I was starting to get fed up of his other women; some of them were so brazen that they would turn up at the house. We used to row a lot and the smile on my face soon became fixed. It was not just isolated incidents but a whole catalogue of abuse. There was no beginning and no end just continuous, never-ending degradation.

I had though, fallen in love with Africa.

One of a number of Beautiful Beaches in Sierra Leone

There is something about the country that gets into your blood. I don't know what it is – whether it is the life style, the atmosphere, the smell; there is no neutrality about it. Freetown had become a home to the children and I and we had made many good friends; not fair-weather friends, but friends that we could love and trust. Friends who did not sit in judgment or pontificate – just warm, caring people who were always there for me. Friends who kept in touch when I returned to England and who still keep in touch with me. Time has no relevance; it was in Freetown that I made my lifelong friends.

Winston and his women – if I were to tell you of every single situation, every incident, we would never finish this story. It is enough to say that he caused me both physical hurt and heartache. I remember one particular time when he brought this woman, Efua, to the house. She was the daughter of the preacher at the local church. Winston would insist on Paul and Cris accompanying Efua and himself to church. He insisted on this most weekends – never asked Adele and Robert – probably because he did not want to be bothered with them; it was always Paul and Cris. Some of my friends knew about this and after church would drive behind him all the way to her house. This was to shame him, but it never worked – in fact it just increased the violence towards me.

Besides the account at the shop, I had no independent money to spend. I could not treat myself, or the children, not even to an ice cream – he made me beg for money, and would then calmly tell me that I couldn't have any. The only way I kept my sanity was through my friends; they would talk to me, sometimes tell me that I was too soft, but were always there for me. This used to make him mad, really mad because some of these people had been his friends and now treated him with contempt. He tried hard to humiliate me in front of friends, people like Bami, Omo, Valerie, and Sudie (the wife of his ex-school teacher) He would tell them lies about me, tell them that I had been a whore in England where I drank and ill treated the children, but they did not believe him. At one time he actually made a list of people I could not see or talk to – all my friends were on that list, including Bami and his family. When I refused to do this he warned me that he would sort me out in a way I would never forget. Winston was always full of threats and I had learnt to ignore them. Not because they were empty threats but because I simply did not have the energy to speculate on what form his latest cruelty would take. If it was to happen it would happen – my energy had to be saved for my children.

I should have picked the danger signs when suddenly, I was no longer expected to entertain his clients'. He did not say anything; it simply stopped happening. One of my lifelines had simply disappeared – I should have seen it coming. He often wasn't home nights and I was tired of asking; I just accepted it. I guess I did not expect him to go to the lengths he did because I foolishly thought that he would not want to shame his family. I did not know that his father was like him; or should it be the other way round? His mother had to put up with the same humiliation and pain; there were no boundaries. Winston would do what he liked; the children and I were his property and he could discard us like old shoes.

The situation between Winston and me went from bad to worse – it felt as if I had been caught up in some kind of tornado that was spiralling at a nightmarish pace. And there seemed nothing that I could do to slow it down. Incident followed incident – and there were no depths to my humiliation. It was just there with me all of the time … hovering, looming, taunting.

My weekly routine was that on every second day I would go into Freetown to the store to do my shopping. This was the store that we had an account with. I would meet one of my close friends – Bianca – there, and we would go for a coffee in the cafe upstairs. It was always Bianca who treated me, but she did it in such a nice way that I felt okay about it. Anyway I valued my time with her. She was one of the friends that Winston did not want me to have contact with. But she was a strong woman and did not care what he said, but was always discreet for my benefit. One day I went to the store to do my food shopping. After signing the bill, Bianca and I went for our usual cup of coffee. When we were ready to leave, one of the shop workers took my groceries to load them into her car. We were standing at the car chatting away, when the shop manager came out with the shop worker. He looked really embarrassed but this did not register with me. I greeted him cheerfully, asking him how he and his family were. Bianca must have noticed his embarrassment because she gave my arm a slight touch and asked him what we could do for him. He would not focus on my face and with his head slightly bent, he told me that Winston had closed the account and he could not let me have any goods. I was shocked and his embarrassment became my embarrassment. I did not know where to look; I just wanted the floor to swallow me. Bianca was furious and told me that it was time to stand up to Winston; I should not let him get away with this behaviour. He had to provide for his children.

I just said, "not now Bianca. Please not now". All I wanted to do was to save face. The manager must have noticed my discomfort and softened slightly as he told me that I could keep the goods in the car but I needed to just sort it out with the Accounts Section. I was so relieved as I was spared the humiliation of having the goods removed from the car. Bianca accompanied me to the Accounts Section. The person behind the counter was none other than Winston's woman, Efua. She was cold and hard and treated me as if I were dirt. She point blank refused to let me take the goods in the car. Bianca offered to pay for them. But Efua still said "No!" I was just standing there trying so hard not to break down. It was as if my body was there, but my spirit was hovering elsewhere. I could not find any words. I could not feel a thing. I just stood there as if carved of stone. From a distance I could hear Bianca urging me to hit Efua, but I had nothing left within me. I just turned and left the shop. Bianca ran after me. I could not speak to her. We got into the car and drove away.

Half way to Banana Water my body started to shake and huge dry sobs racked my body. Bianca had to stop the car and I stuck my head out of the door and was sick. It was as if I needed to get rid of poison in my body. Bianca just held me; quietly soothing me. When I had calmed down she tried to say to me that I needed to stand up for myself, fight for myself; not let Winston walk all over me.

All I could say was, "You do not understand, none of you know what he is capable of. I do not have the strength to fight, I am so tired, so very tired." I knew that Bianca was worried for me, but I told her that I would be all right, I just needed some time to myself. That evening when Winston came home to change before going out for the evening, I confronted him. I was so angry that I forgot that the children were within earshot. We had an almighty row with me shouting and choking on my anger at the same time. He slapped me across my face and as it echoed I suddenly saw Paul make a lunge at Winston. Before I could do anything he was laying into Paul. I thought he was going to kill him. I tried to get between with no luck as he shoved me aside. He suddenly stopped and left the house. I knew that he would not be back that evening.

As I cleaned my eldest son's face, I thought what the hell was I doing. My children were important to me but I could not protect them. What was I trying to prove by staying with this man? Paul was now at age where he always tried to protect me; this meant that he often felt his father's fists. I should be able to protect him. I was nothing but a selfish, pathetic mother and I hated myself, I hated my weakness, I hated the fact that I still loved this brutal man, and I hated my inability to protect my children – all I could feel was desperate hate for myself. And in spite of everything I still did not leave this man!

* * *

It was at this point that I really wanted to ask Betty, "WHY?" I could feel her pain and her children's pain and it was so very hard not to judge her. I had thought that I was able to understand where she was coming from – and part of me did – but there was another part that struggled to understand. How bad did things have to get before she decided to leave Winston? In a lot of ways I had learned to handle the violence and abuse to her but could not deal with it when he directly targeted the children. I guess, that if there were a therapist around, s/he would try to explain it by saying it was "projection". In doing this story with Betty I had come to love and respect her. The bottom line was that there always would be a bridge I would never be able to cross – the only way was to have been with her physically when the violence and abuse happened. But I felt that I needed to say something about how I was feeling.

The moment the words came out of my mouth I regretted it. A shadow engulfed her eyes as she said, "Do you not think that I have asked myself this a hundred times over? My children are now adults and I am so proud of them. In spite of me, in spite of everything they have made something of themselves. But underneath their cloaks of success, are deep scars, some healed and some still raw. And I put those scars there, I am equally responsible and I have to live with this. Looking back, I cannot believe that I had convinced myself that everything I did was for the children – they were my life, they were like the breath in my body, but I have to live with the knowledge that I let them down."

Seeing her visible pain, I was angry with myself. Betty was not asking me to understand or even to accept, she was just telling me her story, the way it was. No embellishments, no justifications, just telling me the way it was. She had let me into her world, not as a social worker or a counsellor, but as a friend. I had to respect this and respect her struggle for survival. I also knew that to apologise was inappropriate so I went over to her and simply hugged her. Tears trickled down her cheeks, she cried. I could not help myself and cried with her.

Once we had calmed down we both laughed at being "silly women"; laughter that was necessary to carry on. Betty continued with her story.

* * *

After that row Winston started buying the food. It was what he called the "basics". This was a bag of potatoes, a tin of milk, a loaf of bread, and if we were lucky a small portion of meat. And I was expected to feed us all on this. He did not eat with us so he was not affected. If I was still doing the entertaining I could have hidden food away for the children. But I no longer had that diversion. And I did not bother to ask him where he was doing his entertaining.

My friend Sudie lived in an area called Murray town. It was walking distance from our house. Sudie knew about my predicament and suggested that as the boys needed to go past her house to get to school, on the way home they could stop at her place on the pretext of playing with her children. They could then eat with her children and Winston would never know. This was because although Winston would not give us enough to live on, he did not want anyone to help us. I was grateful to Sudie as it meant that I could stretch the little food we had to feed Adele, Robert and myself.

I do not know how but Winston found out about this arrangement. To teach us a lesson he stopped paying the bills. This meant that in a short time we had no electricity. Can you imagine what it was like? In Africa the nights descend on you suddenly – to have no light, cooking facilities or hot water was really scary. I never expected him to stoop so low; forget about me, but depriving his own flesh and blood. To have no electricity meant that not only did we have no light, but we also had no cooking facilities and no fridge. In Africa because of the heat we needed the fridge to keep food fresh. I could handle not having lighting; there were always candles and oil lamps. The children could treat the situation as some kind of an adventure. But firstly not to have access to money so as to buy suitable food and then not to be able to cook it just tested my endurance.

My friends were wonderful and rallied round me. They knew not to offer me money as it would have really upset me – so they helped me in other ways. Somebody provided me with candles, which was a relief. We sometimes had problems with snakes and I was terrified that the children might step on one in the dark. I had tried to plead with Winston but he just laughed at me. So I was dependent on the kindness of my friends. It did not stop at candles – somebody found me a calor gas stove so at least we could boil water and do some cooking. Paul, Cris, Adele and Robert all started going to Bianca's and she would feed them with her children. There was no sense of accepting charity – it was just treated as part of our routine.

On one occasion, my next-door neighbours, who were Italians, sent me a crate of fish. They owned a fish factory and must have heard about my predicament. I did not have the courage to tell them that I had no fridge, so I ended throwing away most of the fish. Bami also gave me some financial help that enabled me to keep the children at school. Winston also refused to pay for their school uniforms etc. He said that as far he was concerned they could go barefoot to school. It was bad enough to shame me but to put the children through such humiliation was sheer cruelty.

I know that Adele had a hard time at school – she had to face taunts from the other children and some of the teachers picked on her for not having a proper uniform. I could not go to school and tell them about our life of hell so she just had to try and put up with the taunts and jeers. Did Winston care or even feel embarrassed that half of Freetown knew his business – knew what he was doing to us? Not a jot; he just laughed and mocked me. However once he found out that the children and I were actually coping and that he could not influence or threaten my friends he stopped laughing and became really vicious.

One day he came home in the early evening. I was surprised, as I had got used to not seeing him for days. In a lot of ways I did not mind as when he was at home, we usually rowed with him ending up beating me. Paul has a lot of memories of this time – this is because Winston found him a threat. When he used to start hitting me Paul would come between us. Winston would then throw me out onto the verandah and lay into Paul, punching him as if he was some kind of a punch bag. The others were terrified of him and tried to keep out of his way. Anyway, what did I start to say? Oh, yes - he came home one evening and brought with him loads of food, chocolates and drinks. He called us into the living room. He had spread the food all over the floor. When we saw the food and drink, my heart started beating – I thought that our punishment had come to an end and that he was now trying to be nice. I am sure that the children felt the same – Paul had no emotion on his face but Cris, Adele and Robert's eyes were all lit up. I remember Robert going towards Winston and asking him for some chocolate. Winston just laughed at him and shoved him aside. He then told our house servant to take all the food, chocolates and drinks and put them back in his car. He then simply drove away.

I was shaking with anger; beatings, abuse, taunts, I could take but to behave in this way to innocent children was disgusting – he was a callous cruel animal. If I had had a gun on me I would have shot him without a qualm. My abuse and humiliation was now also the children's abuse and humiliation. I was no longer sure as to whether I could protect them.

I know that it might seem to you that all I had; all I experienced was just pain – it often felt like that most of the time. There were some good times as well. In spite of all that they faced, all my four children really blossomed in Africa. In lots of ways they had the experience of meeting and being close to lots of different African people. This meant that they no longer had to think that all men were like their father.

Looking back, in lots of ways I was glad that we had come to Africa. It helped us develop another view of the world – a view we would never have got in the European world. I often wonder whether it is the African experience that really gave my children the strength to be survivors and not simply victims. I will never know but can only speculate; in my heart I wanted to believe that I had got something right, that I had not totally failed them. We did have some memorable good times. This was all due to my friends. They used to invite us out, invite us to their parties but never included Winston – and this used to make him mad. He did not want them doing anything for me, even giving me a lift. But he could not control them and this used to really bug him. He could not bear the fact that in spite of everything I was able to enjoy myself and tried to have fun in a grim situation.

I remember going to see Ebu's wedding (Ebu was Sudie's sister). He was not invited and he was furious. The children looked so smart in their outfits, and I looked good in mine. Seeing us dressed up, if you had not known the truth, you would never have guessed about our sordid lives. We had a great time at the wedding. The music was great and there was lots of food. I had to stop Cris and Robert pigging themselves. People were all so warm and accepting of us; if they were talking about us behind our backs there were no signs, no embarrassed silences or sudden change of conversation. I had become an expert in working out if we were being gossiped about.

It was outings like this, where I could let my hair down and dance away the night that helped me hold onto my sanity. It not only gave me renewed faith in human nature but it also gave me the strength to survive, come what may.

Winston was getting really frustrated at being left out of what he considered his circle of friends. He just could not bear the fact that many of them were loyal to me. His immediate family did not want to get involved and so kept their distance. Anyway I had heard through the grapevine that his father was very like him. In fact people often said, "like father, like son". I would have liked to get close to his mother, but she seemed terrified and I did not want to do anything which would incur the wrath of both father and son.

One night I visited Bianca and she insisted on driving us home. When we got there I saw his car in the yard. Bianca wanted to come in with me but I told her that I would be all right; I knew that Winston would get even angrier if he saw Bianca with me. I told the children to go straight to their rooms. Paul and Adele wanted to stay with me but I told Paul to go and get the younger children to bed.

Winston was waiting for me. I knew instinctively by his stance that he was going to beat the living daylights out of me. When this used to happen, I wanted it to happen quickly. It always felt as if my spirit had left my body and all that was facing him was an empty body. My spirit was invisible; floating around, wanting him to get it over and done with. But it always felt as if my spirit was laughing at Winston; he always thought that he was battering and punishing my body and spirit, but my spirit always escaped, only returning to my body when he had finished. That night he not only beat me but also gave me a good kicking. In my stomach … I could not breathe; in my side… I could not stand; and then finally in my face... and he injured my eye. He left me with blood all over my face and it was Paul who got help and cleaned and comforted me.

Next day Sudie came to see me. In the middle of her visit he came home. I know that Sudie saw the terror in my face because she whispered, "Betty don't worry, I will keep my mouth shut." When Winston saw her, his face contorted with rage and seeing that, Sudie could not stop herself. She challenged him and called him some nasty names. He just told her to get out of his house. She calmed down and in a cold voice I did not recognise she said, "You can stop me from coming to your house but you cannot stop Betty from coming to my house. My doors will always be open to her and the children. But not to you!" And she walked out giving me a gentle hug.

I expected havoc, but he just looked at me and walked out, not returning for a few days. By now I should have known that he was not going to forget or forgive me for "showing him up" in front of Sudie. Not that I did anything, he did it all… but it always seemed to be my fault. Soon after he came home and threw some pieces of paper on the table. They looked like tickets, so I tentatively reached out for them. He said, "Read them – I want you to read them aloud."

As I read them, my hands started shaking and I started to feel like a block of ice... I had to sit down. He made me read through every line on those tickets. Yes, they were tickets; tickets to return to England by the ship called the 'Auriol'. But the tickets were only for Robert, Adele and I. My voice sounded very strange and reedy, "What does this mean?"

"You and your babies are going back to England. My sons are staying with me. You have disrupted my life, acted like a slut, and I have had enough ...You are going to your home... but Paul and Cris will stay with me." I was stunned. He could not do this... but he did. I cried, grovelled, literally kissed his feet but I was to lose my two sons. He had at last found the one sure way to get at both my body and spirit – I was crushed.

I cannot remember what I said to the boys – what could I say? All I can remember was their eyes – that look of pain and disbelief I will carry to my grave. I will never forget their eyes. Cris cried but Paul just became hard and cold. He kept saying to me that whatever happened he would look after Cris, he would look after Cris with his life...

I had no words left, no explanations, no justifications. It was a nightmare. My friends could not believe it. Bami tried to talk to Winston, but he would not budge. I must have packed – I can remember him constantly rummaging through my packing, checking what I was taking.

I wrote to my sister-in-law to tell her that I was coming back to England (whilst in Africa I had re-established contact with my brother, but he had since died). By the time we left I had not heard from her so I assumed that she would be meeting us and offering us temporary accommodation I cannot find the words to describe my anguish when it was time to say good-bye to Paul and Cris. Friends had quietly given me some money and reassured me that they would keep an eye on the boys. But we had never been separated, except for that one time in England. I am not even sure that Adele and Robert had fully understood what was happening – I myself felt that I would get up and discover this was all a horrible dream.

We left the shores of Africa and were at sea on the Auriol for ten days. My heart was breaking; a part of me was shattered into pieces and left with my two sons; but I had to continue, pretend I was all right for the sake of Robert and Adele. I simply cannot find the words. There are no words to describe a breaking heart; no words to describe my anguish. That bastard had crushed a part of me that would never be whole again. My spirit was no longer smiling... it had gone absolutely still...trapped by my anguish.

Return to England

"...Cold grey skies welcomed us...it was a reflection of how I felt inside...38 years old...separated from my two sons...two children with me...no income...no home...just coldness and greyness".

The 'Auriol' docked into Liverpool and it felt strange to be back, but this time with only half my family. Adele and Robert were keen to go ashore so we were scuttling around our cabin getting our things together. An announcement came over the tannoy but I was too engrossed with sorting out our baggage so I paid no attention. It was Adele who said, "Mum, I think the message is for you – they want you to go and see the Captain". This time I listened to the announcement and it was the Captain wanting me to go to his office. What on earth for? Was there another unpleasant surprise from Winston? I needed to go and find out. I told the children to stay put and not to leave the cabin until I returned. They wanted to come with me but I told them sharply that they had to wait for me. If I was to get another dose of nastiness I did not want them to see me upset. They already had to put up with a lot, and I did not want to burden them further.

When I got to the Captain's office there was a man waiting for me. He told me that he was from Welfare; I guess that he was some kind of social worker. My sister-in-law had contacted his office to say that she could not offer me accommodation. I was devastated – why had she not written to me instead of leaving me in this predicament. What was I to do? Even in England we were not wanted. I felt really weary and just said to the man, "I have nowhere to go and very little money. I have two children with me – I guess I need your help". He said that he had been aware that I would not have anywhere to go so he had reserved some bed space in a Homeless Families Hostel in Liverpool. As they say "beggars cannot be choosy," so I collected the children, our baggage and accompanied this man to the hostel.

After being used to the warmth of the African sun, Liverpool felt chilly. The smells were so different form that of Africa – they were cloying and unwelcoming. When we arrived at the hostel, I had to swallow hard and put on a cheerful face for Adele and Robert. The place looked like old stables which had been converted to living accommodation. Very apt, do you not think? When we went inside it was just as dreadful. There was a horrible stench, like rotting cabbage and the place was dark and damp. Adele and Robert clutched each of my hands and I could feel their rapid breathing against my arm. Our room was no better and all I could do was thank the man for his help. After all it was not his fault…and I had always been able to make sure we had decent living accommodation.

We were there for about two days when I decided we had to find somewhere else. The children were being tormented by other children and the name calling was getting me down. You had to watch your back all the time but more importantly I needed to get a job. Although I had money with me, and I had to silently thank my friends for this, it was not going to last. I decided to go back to Manchester as it was familiar ground and I knew my way around. I also knew that I had an aunt there. So I phoned my sister-in-law and after a few polite pleasantries I asked her if she had my aunt's address. She did and she also told me my aunt lived on her own in a large house and would probably put us up. After that call I felt a bit hopeful.

I knew why my sister-in-law would not have us. Quite simply it was because my children were black. There were no guarantees that my aunt was not just as bigoted but I hoped that living in Manchester might have changed traditional white views.

Rather than write to her and risk a rejection I decided to go and see her in Manchester. She was not exactly welcoming but when she heard about my predicament and also that I would pay for our board, she agreed to have us as 'paying guests'. I was so relieved – at least we now could get out of that hostel and try to sort out our lives together again, in some semblance of normality.

Moving back to Manchester was such a relief. I hoped to be able to make contact with some old friends but first I needed to do the necessary things. Like getting the children into school and finding a job. The children were old enough to look after themselves but there needed to be an adult around. My aunt agreed that if I got a job she would keep an eye out for the children.

There was little difficulty in getting both Robert and Adele into school. The area in which my aunt lived was in what is now known as Stamford Street, Old Trafford. It was an area which was culturally diverse although quite heavily populated by the Irish community. I did not feel as though we stood out like a sore thumb so I felt I had made the right decision in coming here. I soon got a job in a local restaurant. As you know, I was not afraid of hard work and was relieved to get work so quickly as it meant I could keep the little money I came with for a rainy day.

My job in the restaurant involved cleaning tables, helping with meals and waiting on tables. It was back-breaking work, long hours and poor pay. But it was a job! The hours of work meant that the children would be home before me. Adele kept insisting that she could look after both Robert and herself until I got home. It was a relief when my aunt said she would see to their evening tea. This meant that they would not have to wait for me to return before they could have their tea. We very quickly got into a routine – we did not talk about Paul and Cris – I was quietly putting money aside determined to fight for their return to me.

Feelings? What feelings? I worked so hard as not to give me time to think. I did not want time to feel. It was safer to be numb. Sometimes at night when I heard the gentle breathing of my two youngest, I would sit on the floor in the bedroom watching them, whilst they were asleep. It was as if their breathing gave me a sense of living – reminded me of the need to survive – it was as if each soft breath was renewing and mending my crushed spirit. So I did not feel, just "did" …

We must have been there for a couple of weeks when I realised that this arrangement was not going to work. My aunt was just as bigoted as my sister-in-law. She had a "colour thing". The house next door to her was empty and she had seen a black family come and view the property. She was terrified of this and had started a local petition which asked the Council to keep "blacks out". I was both furious and upset when I found out about this…but did not challenge her. The children had settled into their school and I did not want to move them again. So I bit my tongue and started quietly looking for alternative accommodation.

Time drifted and we were now in winter. My hours of work made it difficult to house-hunt. I guess at a superficial level the arrangement was working and I did not want to move to grubby accommodation. That is all that seemed available to a single parent with black children. The cold was also getting to me as we did not have suitable clothing and my chest was playing up. I had almost forgotten about my weak chest because I had thrived in Africa. We must have been there for about six weeks; although I wrote every week to Paul and Cris I got no response – it was as if my letters were falling down a bottomless pit and disappearing altogether.

During this time I was missing Paul and Cris like mad. We would do little things or have certain food and often would begin to say, "Paul would have liked this" or "Cris would have… and then have to stop and bite our tongues. I worried for them and even prayed on a regular basis pleading with God to keep them safe. I knew that Bami would look after them but they were still under Winston's control… and the bottom line was that they were not safe. So when I came home one day, weary from a long day at work, and saw a letter with a Sierra Leone stamp waiting for me, my heart skipped a beat.

I had to sit down as I held the letter to my nose breathing in the African smells. It probably smelt like any old letter but I wanted to inhale the smell of Africa, the smell of my two sons.

I recognised Winston's handwriting and this made me take a long deep breath. As I opened the envelope my heart slowed down as it was clear that there were no letters from my sons. All I could see was Winston's scrawl and I was terrified to read further. As I hardened myself I started to read – you could have knocked me down with a feather. He was asking me to return to Africa and said he would send me the fares! Of course there were conditions, like I was not allowed to speak to certain named people. This was literally everyone I knew…but all I could see was this life-line to my sons. I could not believe it and I kept reading the letter over and over again.

It was not a hard decision. Adele, Robert and I missed Africa, my health was playing up in the cold, my Aunt was constantly picking on the children …but most importantly we would be reunited with Paul and Cris. Do not ask me how, but I also managed to convince myself that Winston was missing us and was probably sorry for his behaviour. So I wrote back, agreeing to his conditions, saying my priority was to be a family again and I would try not to upset him. In a couple of weeks the fares arrived and I started making arrangements to leave England once again.

I did not want to waste time – now that I had made the decision to return I wanted it to happen quickly. There was no earthly reason why I should be separated from Paul and Cris a minute longer than necessary. I went to the offices of the shipping company and found that I had just missed the Auriol. The man in the office said that I could wait for its return. But that was time being wasted. He must have seen the frustration on my face – he suggested that the only alternative was to use one of the cargo ships. They would be pretty basic, but I did not care and agreed. We would be sailing for Africa in a couple of days.

I wrote to Winston immediately giving him the details of the ship and the sailing date and scurried around getting ready to go. This time it was as if my feet and hands had wings – I could not stop singing and my infectious mood rubbed off on Adele and Robert. It felt as if we were going on holiday – and the smile on my face was genuine.

We boarded the ship at Liverpool. There were only thirty other passengers who were mostly Nigerians. It took us ten days to get to Sierra Leone. The journey was pleasant and we had some good times on board. The ship did not stop en route so we had to make our own entertainment and we did. It was only as I saw the African shoreline in the distance that I started to panic and worry. What was awaiting me? Had I been too trusting? Had Winston truly regretted his behaviour? What state would Paul and Cris be in? Would they forgive me for leaving them behind?

In spite of my growing doubts, it really felt as if I had come out from a deep nightmare…my whole body was tingling with feeling. There was no sense of dullness around me – everything around me had an edge to it. My spirit felt free and untrammelled – I was just going home to my two sons… Nothing would ever keep us apart again.

As the ship touched the Sierra Leone shoreline, Adele, Robert and I looked for Winston. There was no sign of him… I told them to wait whilst I looked for him. He had not come to meet us. What on earth was going on? I began to think the worst and had to determinedly hold my anxiety at bay. I came back to Adele and Robert and kept the cheerful look on my face saying "I will just go and ring your father; he must have got caught with something…"

Whatever happened, we were back in Africa and no power on earth would stop me from seeing my sons. My spirit was no longer crushed – it was soaring and determined… if a fight was to be had, then a fight it would be. We were indeed back home in Africa and as the heat bounced off the deck, I said to myself – "As God is my witness, no one will ever separate me from my children, not ever!" A silent vow which was to come back and haunt me – a vow that I was to keep!

The Beginning of the End...

"Returning to Africa I just hoped that things would be better. But when I saw Winston I knew that things had not changed. All I could feel was a sense of gratitude for being allowed to be with my sons again...."

* * *

Not seeing Winston ashore, I went to a phone and contacted him at work. He was expecting us the next day – it seemed that we had arrived a day early. Anyway he said to stay put and he would be down to the harbour to pick us up. True to his word he turned up soon after.

When we got to his car we saw a strange child sitting in the front passenger seat. This was the child of one of his women. Was I not even allowed some short time of fantasy – some time to at least start believing in being family again? If the presence of the child was to give me some kind of message that things had not changed, then he had succeeded. I felt bitter that I was not even allowed the opportunity to save face. He made all the children sit on the back seat.

Once he started the engine of the car, I asked him what he was playing at. He looked at me with such viciousness. The welcoming smile had changed to a nasty curl of his upper lip. He replied in a voice that the children could hear, "You mind your own business. Do not ever question me; what I do has nothing whatsoever to do with you!" The rest of the journey was conducted in silence.

As the car passed familiar sights, I could hear Adele and Robert identify the familiar. I could not join in. The car sometimes avoided the potholes in the road, and sometimes had no alternative but to drive through some of the potholes. We lurched from side to side, with the smell of the African earth hitting our nostrils. It was hard to believe that ten days ago we were in the throes of winter in England and now all we could feel was the heat of the African sun as it filtered through the open windows. I was oblivious to all this – I just looked out of the window with dull eyes, knowing that my return to Africa was just one of Winston's sadistic games.

I somehow had expected that he would take us to his parent's house. When we drove past their house it was clear that we were heading for Banana Water. I was surprised, as I had thought that he had given up the house. However I knew better than to express surprise, so when we arrived I started unloading the car as if it was something I did every day. I got Robert and Adele to take the hand luggage up to the house, whilst Winston and I took the bigger pieces of luggage. My life had always been packed in suitcases, and like the pain I carried... the cases got heavier with every move.

I had expected to see Paul and Cris; but Winston said that he had sent them to school and they would stop over on their way back from school. Once we had got all our things into the house he grabbed me by my arm and hustled me into the bedroom. I was not expecting this, so when he had grabbed me I struggled... in the bedroom he let me go and I could see the ugly red weals on my arm. He then spoke in a very matter of fact tone – he could have been discussing the weather – his voice was quiet. But then, he never had to speak loudly to intimidate me – it was when he spoke softly but every word was like the sound of a whiplash bouncing off my bare back, that I knew serious trouble was brewing.

He said, "You see those marks on your arm; I can do that at anytime and there is no one who can stop me. Let us get one thing straight; I have not brought you back because I want you – simply because I need someone to look after the boys. You are here so that I can punish you; punish you for all the disgrace that you have brought to my family name. Just remember, as far as I am concerned, you are nothing but a slut...a whore bearing my family name."

What could I say – this was my welcome home. I wanted him out of my sight; I cannot remember what I felt or what I thought at the time. There was just this sense of hysteria bubbling inside of me – like a boiling pot of water, desperate to spill over, to escape; but the sides of the pot were too high and there was no escape. I could not afford to bubble dry, so I kept a tight hold of my emotions and just waited for him to leave.

As soon as he left I walked around this familiar house – it was just a house – it was not my home. There were no bars on the windows and I had the keys to the locks on the doors. There was nothing to stop me from walking out never to return. But Winston's words had placed a cage around me – I was and I felt trapped. He needed no locks, no bars... his words alone were enough. Like a caged animal, I knew that there was no escape unless the 'master' wished it so – and like a caged animal I had to learn to play the game or I would not be allowed to survive.

That evening I was reunited with my sons. It was an emotional reunion – but even with the tears in my eyes I could see my pain reflected in my sons' eyes. They held onto me as if I was their life blood – and in a lot of ways we were indeed, each other's sustenance and life blood. They seemed taller and I despaired at the hardness in Paul's eyes. But perhaps this is their story to tell ... I felt as if I had betrayed them, and I was afraid of what they would tell me. Cris has since said that he would never have survived without Paul – but that is their story, not mine. I just thanked God that we were all together again.

Life went on ... it was as if I had never left Africa. In spite of his rules, my friends still insisted on seeing me. We were just careful not to throw this back in Winston's face. Bianca and Sudie would have liked to have confronted him, but for my sake helped me play the "game". We had an account in a shop in town and could get groceries to feed the children and myself. They used to bill us at the end of the month and with the help of friends I always managed to pay the bill. Winston made no effort to do so and did not make any attempt to give me money on a regular basis. He sometimes felt generous and would give me cash that I would hide away and pretend that I had spent. I had to do this or else, once his generous mood had passed, he would have tried to take the money off me.

My relationship with Winston was like being on a roller coaster, with highs and lows. I knew that he had several women friends that he kept company with. We would not see him for days and he would then appear, either in a good mood or in a bad one. It was often the latter but it did not matter what his mood was, he always "used" me sexually. I say "used" because there was never any emotion, never any gentleness... it was a mechanical act – I had to perform my wifely duties! Many a night I spent crying myself to sleep... that is all I seemed to do – cry! After he finished using me I always had to go for a bath; it became a ritual. The bathroom gave me some space but I also felt the need to scrub away any memory of his physical contact with me.

The one thing that constantly reminded me that I had been away from Africa was Paul and Cris. Paul had become a little distant – before, he had always been someone I could talk to. Looking back now I feel so bad because I feel I "made" him grow up too quickly. He was a child and I often forgot this. Every time I looked at him, I could see hurt in his eyes; and all I could hope was that time would heal the scars that both Winston and I had inflicted on this sweet innocent child. Cris, on the other hand, was very clingy. He always wanted to be near me and would get really very anxious if I was out for too long. Both children used to have nightmares – a constant reminder that I had failed them. I also had to balance their needs with that of Adele and Robert. Although they had been with me, they too carried pain and every time I looked at my four children I felt the guilt of having let them down. I still carry this guilt around with me – it is like a heavy boulder in my body. There is no way of getting rid of it... even looking at my children today, and being thankful that they are all doing well... the guilt was my burden.

Why could I not have been strong and stood up to Winston? I had no fight left in me... all I could do was cry. But tears never washed the pain and guilt away; this was a stain, a burden I would always have with me and within me. My friends used to stay that I used to just lie down, quite literally, and let Winston walk all over me. "Fight, Betty, fight" they would say; but all I could do was cry... and cry... and cry. There was no beginning and no ending to the tears, the guilt, and the pain.

It was not long before Winston started his old tricks of humiliating me in public. Things like closing the account at the shop and going to church with his women friends. Refusing to take me with him to parties, and then getting mad that I was invited in my own right. There was no end to the humiliation and the abuse. Things steadily started getting very bad. He started moving things, furniture out of the house; not paying the electricity bill. It was about this time that I started hearing rumours about him. Of course he never told me what was going on; perhaps he knew that I would not believe him. Sudie told me that she had heard members of his family talking about him. She only told me about the rumours when I told her that the police had turned up and had insisted on searching the house. I did not have a clue as to what they were looking for and they would not answer my questions. They told me to speak to my husband and said that for the present he was being detained. Detained for what? No answer. I went to see Sudie and asked her whether she knew what was going on.

I was really distraught and kept saying how ashamed I was that the whole neighbourhood, if not the whole of Freetown would soon know about the police visit. Sudie calmed me down and told me that she had heard that the Cement Company, his employer, suspected him of embezzling money from the Company. This did not surprise me – after all he had a history of dishonesty. It seemed that he was first suspended; and I wondered whether this was why he had closed the account at the shop, and was refusing to pay the bills. However I was never clear as to what had happened, but only knew that he had once again wormed his way out of a corner – the case never went to Court.

I could not discuss this with him as he assumed I did not know, and it was easier to pretend that I did not have a clue about his activities outside our house. All that I was aware of was that he was going to take his frustration out on us; little did I suspect to what lengths he would go. Talk about the ostrich putting its head under the sand. I knew that things would get bad, but my imagination failed to stretch, failed to really accept what kind of a man he really was. I thought that I had seen the worst of what he could do, but I was to learn that hate and vengeance had no boundaries, no limits. Cruelty was like a flooding river, with no banks to hold it He was going to surpass himself and I was to be tormented to breaking point. And the only fight left in me was my useless tears.

One day a strange man came to the door and asked me if I was "Mrs. Beatrice Jones". As one would, I said, "Yes, I am Mrs. Jones. What can I do for you?" A common enough statement – I was being polite. He handed me a letter and asked me to sign for it. I did not check what I was signing, but just signed it thinking that I was signing for receipt of the letter. When he had left I went into the house and opened the letter. As I read the contents of the letter I had to sit down. I cannot remember, but one of the children's voices penetrated through the waves of shock. I heard them asking if I was all right. I have no memory of my reply – all I can remember are the words in that letter bouncing up from the sheet of paper, having a wild dance in front of my eyes.

The letter was from Winston saying that he was taking the children to his mother's. He said that I was an unfit mother and wife. By signing for the letter, it seemed that I had given my consent to this move. The letter said that there was no place for me and I could do what I liked – but the children were going with him. They were his children and therefore his responsibility. I tried to laugh at this hollow mockery of responsibility but no sound passed my lips. I somehow just could not pull myself together; I just sat there, the children's voices in the distance – just sat there watching the bottom fall out of my world; spiralling away from me – and I could not do a thing to stop it.

I really do not know how long I sat there, with wave after wave of numbness washing over me – my face felt damp – I did not even know that tears were flowing liberally over my cheeks. The thing that brought me out of my daze was the sound of a car in the drive. I thought that it was Sudie or Bianca so I went out to welcome them. It was Winston! I was shocked – I did not expect to see him so quickly – as the thought flashed through my mind that he must have been parked on the road waiting for my signature on that fatal piece of paper, I also realised that he had caught me unprepared.

He shouted to the children to pack their things; they looked at me. but I had no words. He then started shoving all the furniture into one room and locked the door. In our bedroom he threw all my belongings into a suitcase, jammed it shut and threw it out into the drive. Oh yes, there was plenty that I could have done during this time... how often have I gone over this... over and over and over... but I let him bundle the children, my children, into his car and watched him drive away. I did nothing to stop him! Standing in the drive, the house locked up behind me, my first thoughts were ... no money, no job, no home. I just stood there trying to marshal up my thoughts, desperately trying to think of what to do next.

I automatically went to see my friend, Valerie, who lived across the road. She asked me no questions; she simply listened to me and agreed to keep my case until I had sorted something out. She told me that I could stay with her, but I did not feel comfortable about taking advantage of her kindness. There was a voice in my head that kept saying, "Go to Sudie, she will tell you what to do. She always knows what to do. She is not weak like you..." And so I went to Sudie's home. Fortunately she was home. I must have looked a state; she just held me in her arms and asked me what had happened. It almost felt as if I was on automatic pilot, but without emotion I told her what happened and kept repeating the words in the letter. She must have sat me down because all I remember was the heat of a hot cup of tea searing the palms of my hands, and hot sweet tea trickling down my throat. That seemed to do the trick – the hot tea seemed to thaw me out of my frozen state. Tears just flowed unchecked down my cheeks.

As my body shook with the force of the tears, she held me and said I had to stay with her. "Betty, I could easily put a knife through him, but that won't be any use. You must start fighting back... you have to start fighting back..." And all I could do was cry, with Sudie's voice echoing in the background, "You must fight..."

Sudie made up the bed in her daughter's bedroom and said that I could use it. I knew that her daughter was in the States but I did not want to take Sudie's generosity for granted. I also felt awful that I had to ask for help but desperation knows no pride. As we were making up the bed I told her that I would try and sort things out as soon as possible and hopefully get out from under her feet. She told me not to be silly, to wash my face and put on my "war paint" and we were going to see Bami.

Once I had freshened up I felt more human and ready to do battle. We went to Valerie's house to pick up my suitcase and I told her where I would be. From there we went to Bami's – my fingers were tightly crossed throughout that drive. He just had to be able to help us. When we got to Bami's house he welcomed us but I could see from his face he was a little guarded. I did not know why but I also did not want to ask; I wanted to believe that he would help me.

As Omo made us drinks I told them what had happened. I was watching Bami's face all the time and saw how serious it got when I said that I had signed a piece of paper I had not read. Although I continued with my story, any lingering hope I had had sunk beyond rescue. I almost knew what he was going to say but got a little distracted with Sudie's exclamations and statements of anger that were like short staccato bursts of a shotgun. Every time I stopped to catch my breath the "shot gun" would go off – if it weren't such a serious situation, it would have been almost comical.

Bami started explaining the law in Sierra Leone – I stopped listening once he had said that the father always had rights of custody. The words just kept echoing in my head.... father has custody... father has custody. There was nothing he could do unless I tried to reconcile with Winston. I think he was genuinely sad about not being able to help me. He offered to pay my passage back to England and said that he would keep an eye on the children... see that they were okay. Oh, Bami tried hard to persuade me that that was my only option. I respected him but could not accept what he was saying – there must be another way. I was not going to leave the country; leave the children with a father who did not care for them...a father who only saw them as possessions. I might have considered Bami's suggestion if I felt that Winston loved his children – but I knew that to leave them with him was to desert them, and I had vowed to never do that again.

We thanked Bami and left for Sudie's house. All the way Sudie gave vent to her frustration and anger, saying men were all a waste of space. I was too tired and when we got to her house I said goodnight and made my way to my room. As I lay in the darkness – there was something soothing about the darkness – I started to plan what I was going to do. All night my head went round and round with ideas and I was grateful for the early morning light. It gave me the excuse to be up rather than pretend sleep; another day meant another chance to get my children back.

I must have been at Sudie's for about a week and a half. Winston would not hear of me seeing the children and I was getting desperate. What were the children thinking of me? Did they believe that I had just deserted them? I did not know what lies Winston had told them and his family, but I knew from bitter experience that he had no scruples. Paul, Cris, Adele and Robert were just pawns in another of his cruel games.

Sudie did not have to say anything but I felt that she was getting a little tired of my constant tears. She is a strong woman and could not understand why I did not just confront him and shame him in public. But then she did not really know what he was capable of! I could not tell her about every sordid detail of my past. We talked about it and she reluctantly agreed that I should move in with

Bianca and her husband. This made some sense and it also meant that Sudie and her husband were no longer in an awkward situation with the Jones' family.

Bianca was very welcoming and I could talk openly as she was also in many ways an "outsider" – being Italian; she was also able to understand my vulnerability and anxiety about the children's safety. It was while I was at Bianca's that I decided enough was enough. I had tried every conciliatory move and Winston was still adamant that I was not to have any contact with the children.

Looking back now I wonder how the children survived – needing to go to school, knowing that their mother and father were the gossips' dream; everyone in our circle of friends was talking about us... and they had to continue not knowing where their mother was and, God alone knew, how Winston was treating them. It was only once I had decided that I had enough, I thought about the saying, "If Mohammed won't come to the mountain, the mountain has to come to Mohammed!"

I decided to make contact with Winston's mother. Sudie set up the meeting. Winston's mother obviously felt really bad for me but she said she was scared of taking sides. I told her that I was prepared to come and live at the family home on Pademba Road. I would do anything to be with my children. She could see I was hurting and agreed to talk to her husband and Winston. It was a gesture that I had to be thankful for. It was two days before I got a message from her. Until then I was a bunch of nerves, what if they said "no"... what if they agreed. My children seemed so near and yet so far... Please God, help me... this has to work. I then got the message –I could move into the family home! I did not know what to feel. I could not pack fast enough... at last I was to be with my children.

At Pademba Road the children and I were to share a bedroom. It was a small bedroom with a double bed. We would be cramped but I was just happy to be with them. We had had a tearful reunion and I knew that being close, physically close, was important to all of us. Winston was not to share with us and I was grateful for this. To make the most of the space, Paul, Cris and Adele were to share the double bed. Robert and I were to have separate camp beds. The arrangements were not the most comfortable and I dared not think about the cockroaches and other insects. I had to be grateful that I was reunited with my children.

Winston used to sleep in what was known as the front room. He still had his women friends, but I could not allow myself to care. Anyway I was so happy to be with the children that nothing else could burst this bubble. You would have thought that by now I would have been wary of real happiness – whenever I got a taste of it, I was not allowed to savour it – it was always taken away from me. And this is exactly what happened yet again!

One early Sunday morning I was not sleeping very well – the camp bed was uncomfortable and I was getting bad backache. As I was quietly trying to get comfortable, the bedroom door creaked open – it was Winston. I thought that he had come for me so I turned my back to the door and pretended to be asleep. My eyes were tightly shut, praying that he would go away. After what seemed like an age away but must have been minutes, I heard the double bed creak. I thought, "What the hell!" I turned to look at the bed and saw that he had got into the bed and was near Adele. He was taking her pyjamas off. Something just exploded in my brain and I jumped up pulling him off the bed, shouting and screaming. For God's sake, my daughter was only 12 years old. I lost control and pulled and kicked him. Adele must have been terrified because she started shouting and crying for me.

The boys had got up and were trying to pull Winston off me... he had started kicking and hitting with his feet and fists; he also attacked Adele, raining blows down on her defenceless head... The shouting and screaming must have awakened his parents because they were standing at the bedroom door. His mother asked what was going on and I tried to explain to them what had happened, but the words just would not come out right.

In his usual way he got control of himself quickly and gave some plausible explanation about wanting to be close to his children and I had misunderstood the situation and started acting like a mad woman. He only hit Adele and me in order to stop our hysteria. And his parents acted as if they believed him and told me to pull myself together. I could not believe it and as I looked over at Winston I expected to see him gloating. Instead he looked at me with such intense hatred that I felt my body tensing, I will never forget that look, so full of venom and hate. I would like to believe that his parents knew that I was telling the truth and that they were afraid of him but I will never know.

As it was Sunday morning he told his parents that he wanted to get dressed and go to Church. They left us telling us to behave ourselves, behave – what did they mean? Anyway, once they left, Winston went over to get his suit from the rail behind the bed. I must have been sitting on my camp bed trying to get control of my emotions, when he suddenly lurched at me, jumping and aiming at my stomach. Some sixth sense must have alerted me, or perhaps one of the children called out a warning. I managed to just roll over before his body weight struck me on my side. I felt pain but I guess it could have been worse if he had actually got my stomach as he had clearly intended to. He calmly got up, suit under his arm, and said, "I am going to church. When I am back I will sort you out!" He left without a backward glance, leaving a decimated family behind. And I thought… "he probably will also go and receive communion…"

I have little memory of how we got through that fateful Sunday. All that I had imprinted in my mind was Adele's face. I wanted to ask her lots of questions. I knew that we had to move from the house. It was not safe and I would not be able to live with myself if I thought that I had placed my daughter, my sweet daughter, under any more risk. We had to move, but where? That was when I made the hardest decision in my life…when I broke the solemn vow I made when I saw the shores of Africa. There would be no way of finding accommodation for the five of us; we were going to have to separate. I was going to have to leave Paul and Cris behind at Pademba Road, and find somewhere for Adele, Robert and myself. I had to believe that my two oldest sons would be able to look after themselves and would be able to keep themselves safe.

The next day I went to see a second cousin of Winston's – it was Cumbi. I do not know why I approached her – perhaps because she was always kind to me. I told her that I had to move out of the house at Pademba Road but knew that it would be difficult to find accommodation for all five of us. I guess that I was hoping that she would say something like, "What nonsense, you must all come and live with me!" Well, she did not say this. What she did say was that it would be better if we moved in with family; it would be more acceptable; so she offered to put Adele, Robert and myself up at her house. Although relieved at her offer, I had to think of breaking the news to the children.

That evening when they were home from school, I told them that I needed to talk to them. I tried to explain that I would be moving out with Adele and Robert to Cumbi's house, but had to leave Paul and Cris with Winston. How do you find words to tell your children that you have no option but to live apart? How do you justify leaving them with a monster knowing that they might be harmed? Anything I said sounded feeble... it did to me, it must have done to them. I tried to reassure them and said that we were only five minutes away and that I would see them every day. I told them that I was going to save like crazy so that we could all return to England... but these were only words. Their eyes said it all – no words were necessary it was in their eyes...

I left Pademba Road with the heavy knowledge that in some way I had betrayed my sons. I had let them down; there were no words, no explanations, no justifications – there was nothing to make me feel less of a traitor. The move to Cumbi's house was just another move, something that I was particularly good at doing.

I think we must have just moved when I got a message from Winston that a meeting at his mother's house had been arranged. The message simply said that it would be in my interest to attend. What did I make of it? Not much – I wondered whether they were going to ask me to return or leave forever. The one thing that

I did know was that there would be no admission of any fault on Winston's part.

Sudie explained to me that this was probably going to be a family meeting to discuss my children and my future. She strongly advised me not to go alone and that I should go with a man the family respected. I was starting to get really nervous and could not quite understand why the whole family had to be involved. They had never supported or helped me before, so why now? I wanted to refuse to attend but she told me that to not go would be to play into Winston's hands. After discussing it at some length, Sudie's husband Doc Jones insisted that he would come with me. He felt that there would be less chance of the family, particularly Winston, manipulating me! Fat chance. I do not think that anyone really understood what Winston was really capable of...

We all met at the Pademba Road house. On entering the room and seeing Winston and his father and brothers I was really glad to have Doc Jones at my side. I have never felt so humiliated, embarrassed and angry all at the same time. I had to sit and listen to a whole load of lies – how I was a bad mother, how I deserted my two sons, how I was unfaithful to Winston, how I was a bad and uncaring wife and it went on and on and on... It felt as if I was caught up in quicksand, the harder I tried to defend myself, the deeper I sank into a quagmire of lies and deceit. Doc Jones was my only lifeline.

I was determined not to cry, although my insides felt as if someone was hacking away determined to make my body cave in... I could not show them what they were really doing to me. My mind must have started drifting at some point... I was brought back to the present when I heard Doc Jones shouting. He was only a small man;

but he was on his feet shouting at Winston calling him everything under the sun. Winston was as cool as a cucumber. He was cold and deadly. I heard him say that he did not want me and he could do what he wanted with me. No one could stop him and of course, nothing and no one had stopped him before. He was going to keep Paul and Cris and he had a right to them – I could do what I liked with myself and Adele and Robert. His parents were nodding their heads in agreement. Doc Jones suddenly got up and said that we were leaving, there was no point talking anymore and I followed him like an obedient child. We left knowing that I was going to have a real fight on my hands.

It was only once we left the house and I could feel the sun on my back and the cool breeze heralding the night that I began to feel. I started to really feel my torn insides, my body started to shake and shake and shake with sobs, but not a teardrop passed through my eyes. Shaking and heavy sobs racked my body.... I felt as if I were drowning. As Doc Jones small frame supported me, I could hear his voice urging me not to give up. He did not know of the vow I had made to myself when I saw the African shoreline from the Auriol; the vow never to allow myself to be separated from all my four children; the look on Paul and Cris's face when we moved to Cumbi's; the deep sense of betrayal I carried around with me – I knew that I could not give up. However, deep inside me, I felt a deep sense of hopelessness because only I and the children knew what Winston, husband and father, was really capable of.

Sudie and Bianca were determined that I was to fight. Doc Jones said that I had to make contact with the British Embassy and ask for help. Amongst the three of them they decided it was best if

Bianca accompanied me to the Embassy – as two white women we would probably be taken more seriously! Of course whilst all this was going on, I had to try and behave normally with the children. I did not want them to get wind of the impending disaster; there would be plenty of time for all of us to face whatever the reality might be...

As agreed, Bianca accompanied me to the Embassy and demanded to see the Ambassador. Bianca was a strong woman – one did not mess with her. She carried a certain sense of authority – not like me, a bundle of nerves. I owe both Bianca and Sudie a lot; they were really my main anchors of support. The honest truth is that without them at this point, heaven alone knows where the children and I would have ended up – this story would almost undoubtedly had a different ending. In spite of Bianca being very demanding, it soon became apparent that the Ambassador was not around and we had to be satisfied in meeting with his Deputy. He was not much help; he basically said that he could only advise me to see a lawyer. They did not get involved with "domestic matters". He did not have to say anything more; I could see the contempt in his eyes and did not have to guess very hard as to what he was thinking! Bianca must have picked up the same message because she could not wait to get out of the office. Once outside she was furious but also made me laugh when she mimicked the man! She said that we were going to see a lawyer; she was not going to let me give up so easily.

The lawyer we went to see was an old friend from way back when Winston was in the R.A.F. It was a man called Johnny Smythe; he knew Winston and knew about his chequered past, so I did not have to try and convince him to help. He was only too willing and said that I needed to get a form completed and signed by Winston agreeing to me leaving the country with Adele and Robert. I needed to get the form from the Embassy. Why did that Deputy not tell us this? I felt really irritated, particularly needing to see that man again. Johnny also said that there was no chance of getting Paul and Cris to accompany us – we needed Winston's consent. Even taking it to court would not give us any guarantees, and this would also be very expensive. I did not have the money and even if my friends lent it to me, I would never be able to pay them back. It was far too much money; all I could do was hope that Bami or even Cumbi could persuade Winston to let me take all the children with me.

That form became a real bone of contention. Winston would not sign it. He kept saying that he had not received it. I was too scared to go up to the house, particularly since he had threatened to make sure that I would not leave Sierra Leone alive. There was absolutely no chance of him agreeing to Paul and Cris accompanying me. Everything seemed a real mess, and I began to believe that I would indeed not survive Sierra Leone! In the end it was Johnny who took the form and made Winston sign it. He could not get him to agree to let me have Paul and Cris. Johnny's advice was to take the two children and run... he felt that Winston's threats of doing away with me, killing me could be very real. He also told me not to tell Winston when and how I was leaving and to try and do it at a time when Winston would be out and about. How was I to break the news to Paul and Cris? I could not even promise them that I would be back or that I would fight for them from England... these would be lies but tell them I must!

The worst thing in telling them was that I had to tell them not to give their father any sense of my pending departure. You know I can not really remember the impact of telling them. I cannot even remember how I told them or even how I felt. It was something I had to do and it was something I never ever wanted to remember. The final cut; the irreversible breaking of my vow; my inability to keep my promise; a mother's ultimate betrayal – to leave Africa KNOWING my sons were not safe, KNOWING that they wanted to be with me, KNOWING that the cruelty I had experienced at their father's hands was now their cruelty; just KNOWING...

The day at last arrived – my sailing date – my last farewell to Africa. It was a Saturday quite near Christmas. I had decided to choose a Saturday because Winston would be out getting drunk on the Friday night and would be in no fit state Saturday morning. The other reason was that the booking office would be closed until Monday so even if he found out there was not much he could do to stop us from leaving. I would have preferred to have waited for the Spring but it was too dangerous to wait that long, so we were to return to England in time for Christmas and the cold winter would be greeting us. There was something ironic about this – perhaps the coldness mirrored the desperation and frozen feelings lying dormant in me. I could not bring myself to think of the time when I would have to bid my two sons "goodbye", not knowing if we would ever see each other again.

We were to sail on the Auriol and I felt some sense of relief as I knew the ship and some of the crew. I had managed to get some passes for Paul, Cris, Cumbi, Bianca, Sudie and Doc Jones. I had to remind Paul and Cris not to say a word to anyone at Pademba Road for fear of Winston getting to know. Cumbi was to collect them on the pretence of bringing them over to see me, Adele and Robert. This worked a treat and I was grateful for their presence and that of my friends as we stood on the dockside waiting to board the Auriol. In no time we were on deck having put our stuff in our cabin. Around us there were people laughing and crying saying goodbyes to family and friends. The atmosphere was strained around us; there was a certain air of solemnity. I wanted to make lighthearted chatter but the words were lodged in my throat, silencing me. Only our eyes mirrored our pain and grief. It was so difficult – Paul was trying so hard to be the responsible big brother; trying to be brave for the sake of Crispin, Adele and Robert. But I could see the confusion and hardness in his eyes. He did not have to say anything; I just knew how he was feeling.

Crispin, on the other hand, was crying and clinging to me. This was almost a relief; at least one of us could show emotion. The others – Bianca, Sudie and Doc Jones – embraced us, said their farewells and went ashore. I knew that they were giving me some time to say my farewell to the boys. Cumbi was still hovering around trying to comfort me. I looked over to Paul who had not shed a tear and it felt as if he had pulled shutters over his eyes. I could feel Cris clutching me and suddenly something snapped in me. This whole scene was ridiculous – there was no way that I could leave my sons knowing that I might never see them again. I was their mother; had I not already let them down; the numerous separations and reconciliations; my inability to protect them from Winston – and now I was going to leave them, KNOWING what lay in store for them. No... hang the consequences! I whispered to them to go to another deck and to hide in the toilets. Once the ship set sail they were to come to my cabin but had to keep out of sight of the other passengers and the crew. Cris was about to ask me something, and I thought; "not now Cris, just move". Paul sensed my urgency and without any hesitation grabbed Cris and made his way to another deck.

Cumbi was aware of what was going on but simply hugged me goodbye and said that she would pray that everything would be all right. I was glad that she did not lecture me or try to dissuade me – I did not want to hear anything that might make me dither. As she left us on deck, she whispered that she had talked to one of the Nigerian stewards and that he had promised to look after us. There was no time to ask any questions as the voice over the tannoy gave the final warning for friends and family to leave the ship as it was about to sail.

As we stood on deck, Adele, Robert and I we waved farewell to the figures ashore – figures which gradually became smaller and smaller. Figures who were my friends, who supported me unquestioningly, who put up with my whimpering and whinging – friends I would dearly miss.

As the African shoreline became distant, I said my silent farewell to a continent I had grown to love; a continent which gave me friends that renewed my faith in human nature; a continent which embraced my children and gave them a chance to meet others like their father and yet so different from him. I felt a sense of relief and sent a silent prayer heavenwards – I at last had managed to keep my vow; the vow I had made on this very deck – I had all my children with me. I had not deserted them. And there were only six people on board who knew of their presence – Paul, Cris, Adele, Robert and me and the steward; it had to remain this way until it was impossible to return Paul and Cris to Freetown. The chains and shackles held by Winston was gradually being eroded away – I could smell freedom, but I could not revel in it, not until we really knew that we were completely free... not until we sailed past Las Palmas. There would be plenty of time for all of us to savour our freedom – to really be with each other without the sense of perpetual fear and without the threat of Winston's presence.

That evening we were all together in our small cabin, planning how we were going to manage the trip without alerting anyone on board the Auriol. It felt good having all four children with me – something I thought I had lost forever. We were just having a giggle over something Robert said when there was a knock at the door. I told Paul and Cris to get into the cupboards and Adele and Robert to lie on the bed as if they were resting. I opened the cabin door slightly, keeping my body between the door and the inside of the cabin. It was a steward – I was about to tell him I had not rung for him, when I recognised him. My stomach dropped as I realised that this was the steward that Cumbi had spoken to. Dear God, why is it that when things start working out, something comes along and gets in the way? Did I have a big sign on me which, said, "Trouble! Come and get me!"? This man meant certain trouble and I did not want to speak to him in front of the children. I did not want him in my cabin so I told Adele to shut the door behind me and not to open it to anyone. I would be back soon. What was it about this man that made me fearful? I did not tell you this, but he was also on the Auriol when we sailed back to Sierra Leone. He was a real creep and made advances to Adele. She was scared of him, particularly when he tried to get into the cabin with her. I found out and had threatened him with the sack – he now had us in his power. I knew that he was going to make me pay for threatening him but again I naively did not imagine how. He had the keys to an empty cabin and hustled me in there. At first I tried to bluff, pretending I did not know what he was going on about, but that did not work, so I tried the tears, something I was good at. That also did not work. I knew that our lives were literally in his hands and I was going to pay big time!

He said that he wanted two things from me - money and sex! I pleaded with him but he was not having it... and he reminded that we were still near enough to Africa for the Captain to turn around the ship and return Paul and Cris to their father. I would almost certainly be detained! Winston would love it – I had played right into his hands. I asked him how much money he wanted and when he said he wanted two hundred pounds I swallowed hard. That would eat into more than half of the money I had on me. How were we to manage when we got to England? I tried to pretend that I did not have that kind of money and he made to leave. I had to grab him and agreed to pay him but I would only pay him half the amount up front. The other half would be given to him once we had sailed past Las Palmas – he could take it or leave it! I knew that I was playing for time but had to keep a desperate look on my face so that he believed me. For a long moment I thought he was going to say, "No," but when he said "Yes", I let my breath out gently, just feeling an enormous sense of relief.

Thinking we had reached an agreement I made a move to leave the cabin. He asked me where I thought I was going and barred my way. Trying to keep calm I said that I was going to get him his money from my cabin. I can still remember his voice and his hot breath against my face and that horrible look in his eyes. I had seen that once too often in Winston and I knew what it meant. He said that he would accompany me to my cabin for the money but there was a second part of his demands I needed to meet. I could not even offer him extra money as a way out; I did not have it, he made it clear that it was sex he wanted and I had to let him.

There was no way out. My children were all that I had; I had let them down so often, I simply could not let them down again. Paul's face kept coming into my mind – the hardness in his eyes – Cris' sobs, Adele and Robert asking me "Why?" over and over, and not having any answers. My body had been used before; if it was the price I had to pay; and so he had the use of my body and somewhere along a bit of my soul died.

* * *

As Betty talked, tears ran down her face unchecked. I went over to her and held her. In between heart wrenching sobs she said, "What will my children think of me? I have never talked about this part of that journey? Are they just going to see me as cheap and weak? How often am I allowed to let them down? The one thing that has kept me going is my Children; they are adults now, but they are still my babies. How are they going to respond to this part of the story?"

What could I say? I wanted to reassure her and I tried but I could not guarantee her anything. I knew two of her children, Adele and Robert, and I could not believe that they would condemn or reject Betty. This was the story of a mother who tried in her own way to fight for the survival of her family, her children. She did not always get it right, but who does? The one thing that clearly rang loud and clear was her love for her children. To give up her body, to allow some stranger exploit every bit of her, surely said in more than words how important her children were. I told Betty to try and talk to them, to prepare them for this part of the story, but I never found out if she did.

She contacted me several months after I had finished talking her story through with her. All she said to me was, "Vera, remember that part of the story when I was on the Auriol returning to England?" I immediately knew what she was talking about; we did not need words to clarify what she meant. "I want you to write it as it happened. Promise?" I wanted to ask her if she had talked it over with her children, or at least with Adele, but could not find the appropriate words. It was her story; her risk and I had to respect this. So I have written it as it was – no embellishments, no drama, just the way Betty told it.

Betty was never able to see the finished story... she was never able to see this part of the story and I feel at a loss, wanting her to see it in print, wanting her to acknowledge her courage, wanting her to see the pride in her children's eyes, just wanting her to be here, to see a dream become a reality but this was not to be. All I can say is that I have tried to be true to her courage and her memory, and I have written it as it was. Hoping like her, not for judgment but for understanding and love.

Betty continued with her story.

* * *

This was a journey we should have enjoyed; we could really have been like a family again. In ten days we would be in hostile and unfriendly England, and yet we were like trapped rats on the ship. I was living off my nerves, what with the increasing demands of that steward, the high spirits of the children – this was a big adventure for them – and the need for me to act normally. I just wanted to get past Las Palmas quickly.

Time has a tendency to drag when you want it to move quickly – and did it drag! We had established a certain routine and became quite good at it. Adele, Robert and I would go for our meals in the dining room. We would carry little plastic bags and when no one was looking would hide food in it to take back to Paul and Cris in the cabin. There was usually loads of fruit and we would buy things like biscuits and crisps from the shop. I used to sometimes see people give us funny looks and if it was not so desperate it would have been funny. They must have wondered where we put all the food that we seemed to demolish at some speed!

Paul and Cris had strict orders that they could only use the toilet when the coast was clear. Even then we took no chances; I insisted on them using my dressing gown and slippers just in case. I remember the people in the next cabin enquiring after me as they thought that I was going to the toilet far too often. It was hard to reassure them keeping a straight face when I could hear and feel the children's stifled giggles behind me. The hardest time was when the woman came to clean out our cabin. I could not risk the boys in the toilet, so we used to bundle them in the cupboard and I would stand against the door pretending to chat to her. If she thought we were a little strange she never said so, but I used to always be terrified that one day one of them would sneeze and the whole "game" would be up!

The person who struggled the most was Cris – I think he resented all this hiding around and could not understand why he could not go and play on deck. He used to really test us all with his constant demands for blankets, pillows and food, in that order. The nights were the best when we could all cuddle up and be really close to each other. It then made everything worthwhile. And as each day went slowly by we came closer and closer to Las Palmas and real danger. Part of trying to act like normal, meant that every night I had to go up to the bar and pretend to socialise. This was hard – I guess this was when I discovered I had a real talent for acting! Perhaps at another level it might have been some relief to spend time with other adults; not to be looking over my shoulder, tensing at every step outside the cabin, trying desperately to hide my anxiety from the children. Whatever the reason, I was able to act as if I had not a care in the world.

It was the night before we were due in Las Palmas. I was desperately worried that that steward would tell on us and that the police would arrest us and send Paul and Cris back to Sierra Leone on the next ship. We were all expected to leave the ship while it was cleaned and refuelled. There was no way in the world that I was going to be able to smuggle the boys off the ship and then back on. I had no place to hide them. It did not even need the steward to tell on us – just the routine would scupper my plans.

I was in the bar with my thoughts going round and round in a circle, desperate to find a way out of this predicament. My guard must have dropped at some point, but I was so deep in thought that when the barman placed a drink in front of me with the compliments of the chief steward I got a fright. The chief steward was also Nigerian, and rightly or wrongly, I was a little wary. He came over to talk to me and in the middle of our conversation he asked me if something was worrying me. I tried to pretend and must admit acted a little coy brushing aside his question. I must have had another drink when he asked me again if something was worrying me. By this point I do not know whether it was the alcohol, whether it was my desperation, whatever it was I took a big chance. Looking back now I really wonder at myself – what made me tell him – maybe it was because I knew that I had nothing much to lose but plenty to gain. They say that the Lord works in mysterious ways. I never quite understood what this meant then, but I do now.

I made him promise not to let anyone know what I was about to tell him. I then poured out my story and told him about Paul and Cris being stowaways, and that I was terrified that they would be found when we docked in Las Palmas. As soon as the words tripped out of my mouth I felt a sense of panic. I had truly messed up now – I could not retract my story. As panic took over I hurriedly excused myself and left the bar making my way to the cabin.

All the way to the cabin I called myself every name I could think of – why could I not be more like Sudie or Bianca? I always let my family down at the most crucial time; perhaps Winston was right – perhaps I was indeed a bad and useless wife and mother. In the cabin I could both feel and hear the gentle breathing of the children. It should have comforted me, but it did not – it made me feel worse.

I do not know how long I sat there with only my thoughts for company when I heard footsteps at the door. As I went to answer the quiet knock on the door, I just felt as if I could see my life flashing by on a roller coaster. With my heart playing a rhythm that, I could make no sense of, I opened the door expecting the worst. It was the chief steward and I immediately thought "someone else wants to use me". You can imagine my surprise when he said that he wanted to help me – I just stood there waiting for the catch! He told me that the ship would be docking in Las Palmas the next night. We would not be going ashore until daylight. He said he would come to the cabin at night and slip a note under the door to let me know it was him. He would then take the boys and hide them in one of the food storerooms. He was the only one with the keys so no-one would get access to the storerooms. I was to act normal and go ashore and he would have the boys back in the cabin once we set sail again. What alternative had I – I had to trust him – so I agreed.

I have never felt so scared; all the time in Las Palmas, trying to buy warm clothing for all the children, I kept wondering whether I had lost the boys for good. There was no way I could tell Robert or Adele what I was thinking so I had to keep on with light conversation, pretending to enjoying myself, all the while desperately worrying, desperately praying for the lives of my two sons.

It worked! When we got back from Las Palmas and once the ship set sail, a knock on the door that evening brought Paul and Cris into my arms. We had done it, and I could not thank the chief steward enough. He just waved aside my thanks and told me to keep them hidden until we were close to England. I could just nod silently, trying so very hard not to cry.

It had always been my intention to tell the Captain that I had the boys on board, but only once I was certain that there was no chance of returning them to Sierra Leone. All four children were on my passport so I knew that legally they would have no problem of remaining with me in England. As we got nearer England the other steward kept pestering me for the rest of the money, saying he would tell the Captain. It was the on the ninth day that I finally told him to take a running jump and that he was not going to get a penny out of me. He could tell the Captain but I felt sure that the Captain would be interested in my side of the story. The venom in his eyes reminded me of Winston and I felt a certain sense of satisfaction to know that for once I had come up trumps! I decided not to wait for him and instead went to see the Captain. I told him the whole story and promised to pay back every penny I owed for the boys' passage. He was incredibly nice and understanding and told me that he would have to inform British Immigration. I left his office feeling an enormous sense of relief. It felt as if all the poison, anxiety and desperation were seeping out of my body slowly but surely. We were truly free!

That evening I knew that somehow the news had filtered out and that people were talking about us. I did not care – I was walking on air – my children and I were free. I knew that England was going to be a hard struggle but I had kept my promise and we were together as a family. We had made it – freedom was beckoning us – there was no going back!

As the *Auriol* pulled into Liverpool Docks the five of us stood on deck, breathing the cold air. Immigration would be waiting for us and a whole new struggle would begin; but we had finally made it. Against all the odds we had made it and I said a silent prayer – someone indeed was looking after me. I knew what was waiting for us, but I believed that I could make a life for us – I had done it before, I could do it again.

British Immigration came on board; they took my passport away and said they would return it only once I had paid up for all the passages. This was not the time to worry about money; I had no home, no job, no income, but we had survived a journey when the odds were heavily stacked against us. We would continue to survive.

As we left the Auriol the chief steward was waiting for us ashore. He gave us a big box and wished us a Merry Christmas! It was a box of fruit! And yes it was Christmas! And my faith in human beings was again renewed; there were good and bad people, and there always was hope for the good to survive. Although the cold bit through our clothes, although we did not know where we were to sleep that night, although we missed the warmth of Africa, although there was a major struggle ahead, it just felt good to be together – our love and determination would enable us to survive. We are and will always be survivors!

She is She
Strong woman
Gentle woman
She is She

Like a candle flame
Sometimes flickering
Struggling to burn bright
She is She

Gentle Stream
Many taking
Always flowing
She is She

Turbulent
Volatile
Sensitive
Sensuous
Caring
Loving
She is She

Always smiling
Joking
Laughing
Teasing
Crying
Ridiculing pain away

Always living
She is She.........

Vera

Betty

Heartache and pain are experienced by most people at some stage throughout their lives - an unfortunate fact of life; but Mum had more than her fair share.

Mum's suffering began as a little girl. She lost her parents at an early age, suffered serious illness while growing up and again early in adult life. She suffered for marrying the man she loved and had to endure the brutality of the man she married.

A lot of the suffering through Mum's early years was probably symptomatic of the times and experienced by many families. The war years, food rationing, malnutrition and with it illness, cut many lives tragically short. Those times had to be endured by many for there was no way out.

There was a way out from Mum's marriage and the brutality of my father. She could have left like a lot of other Mums might have done in the circumstances and who could have blamed her; but not our Mum, she stayed and she stayed for us.

Mum paid the ultimate sacrifice; she forfeited her happiness and her freedom for the sake of her children.

We love you Mum.

Cris

Printed in Great Britain
by Amazon.co.uk, Ltd.,
Marston Gate.